Polished Spiral Karin Kuhlmann

"Although the creation of fractals is bounded to strict mathematical rules, the results are always very inspiring."– **Karin Kuhlmann**

Investigations
IN NUMBER, DATA, AND SPACE®

Glenview, Illinois • Boston, Massachusetts
Chandler, Arizona • Upper Saddle River, New Jersey

T E R C

The Investigations curriculum was developed by TERC, Cambridge, MA.

This material is based on work supported by the National Science Foundation ("NSF") under Grant No. ESI-0095450. Any opinions, findings, and conclusions or recommendations expressed in this material are those of the author(s) and do not necessarily reflect the views of the National Science Foundation.

ISBN-13: 978-0-328-60037-3

ISBN-10: 0-328-60037-7

5 6 7 8 9 10 V064 16 15 14 13

TERC

Co-Principal Investigators

Susan Jo Russell

Karen Economopoulos

Authors

Lucy Wittenberg
Director Grades 3–5

Karen Economopoulos
Director Grades K–2

Virginia Bastable
(SummerMath for Teachers,
Mt. Holyoke College)

Katie Hickey Bloomfield

Keith Cochran

Darrell Earnest

Arusha Hollister

Nancy Horowitz

Erin Leidl

Megan Murray

Young Oh

Beth W. Perry

Susan Jo Russell

Deborah Schifter
(Education
Development Center)

Kathy Sillman

Administrative Staff

Amy Taber
Project Manager

Beth Bergeron

Lorraine Brooks

Emi Fujiwara

Contributing Authors

Denise Baumann

Jennifer DiBrienza

Hollee Freeman

Paula Hooper

Jan Mokros

Stephen Monk
(University of Washington)

Mary Beth O'Connor

Judy Storeygard

Cornelia Tierney

Elizabeth Van Cleef

Carol Wright

Technology

Jim Hammerman

Classroom Field Work

Amy Appell

Rachel E. Davis

Traci Higgins

Julia Thompson

Collaborating Teachers

This group of dedicated teachers carried out extensive field testing in their classrooms, met regularly to discuss issues of teaching and learning mathematics, provided feedback to staff, welcomed staff into their classrooms to document students' work, and contributed both suggestions and written material that has been incorporated into the curriculum.

Bethany Altchek

Linda Amaral

Kimberly Beauregard

Barbara Bernard

Nancy Buell

Rose Christiansen

Chris Colbath-Hess

Lisette Colon

Kim Cook

Frances Cooper

Kathleen Drew

Rebeka Eston Salemi

Thomas Fisher

Michael Flynn

Holly Ghazey

Susan Gillis

Danielle Harrington

Elaine Herzog

Francine Hiller

Kirsten Lee Howard

Liliana Klass

Leslie Kramer

Melissa Lee Andrichak

Kelley Lee Sadowski

Jennifer Levitan

Mary Lou LoVecchio

Kristen McEnaney

Maura McGrail

Kathe Millett

Florence Molyneaux

Amy Monkiewicz

Elizabeth Monopoli

Carol Murray

Robyn Musser

Christine Norrman

Deborah O'Brien

Timothy O'Connor

Anne Marie O'Reilly

Mark Paige

Margaret Riddle

Karen Schweitzer

Elisabeth Seyferth

Susan Smith

Debra Sorvillo

Shoshanah Starr

Janice Szymaszek

Karen Tobin

JoAnn Trauschke

Ana Vaisenstein

Yvonne Watson

Michelle Woods

Mary Wright

Note: Unless otherwise noted, all contributors listed above were staff of the Education Research Collaborative at TERC during their work on the curriculum. Other affiliations during the time of development are listed.

Advisors

Deborah Lowenberg Ball,
University of Michigan

Hyman Bass, Professor of Mathematics and Mathematics Education
University of Michigan

Mary Canner, Principal, Natick Public Schools

Thomas Carpenter, Professor of Curriculum and Instruction,
University of Wisconsin-Madison

Janis Freckmann, Elementary Mathematics Coordinator,
Milwaukee Public Schools

Lynne Godfrey, Mathematics Coach,
Cambridge Public Schools

Ginger Hanlon, Instructional Specialist in Mathematics,
New York City Public Schools

DeAnn Huinker, Director, Center for Mathematics and
Science Education Research, University of Wisconsin-Milwaukee

James Kaput, Professor of Mathematics, University of
Massachusetts-Dartmouth

Kate Kline, Associate Professor, Department of Mathematics
and Statistics, Western Michigan University

Jim Lewis, Professor of Mathematics,
University of Nebraska-Lincoln

William McCallum, Professor of Mathematics,
University of Arizona

Harriet Pollatsek, Professor of Mathematics,
Mount Holyoke College

Debra Shein-Gerson, Elementary Mathematics Specialist,
Weston Public Schools

Gary Shevell, Assistant Principal,
New York City Public Schools

Liz Sweeney, Elementary Math Department,
Boston Public Schools

Lucy West, Consultant, Metamorphosis:
Teaching Learning Communities, Inc.

This revision of the curriculum was built on the work of the many authors who contributed to the first edition (published between 1994 and 1998). We acknowledge the critical contributions of these authors in developing the content and pedagogy of *Investigations*:

Authors

Joan Akers

Michael T. Battista

Douglas H. Clements

Karen Economopoulos

Marlene Kliman

Jan Mokros

Megan Murray

Ricardo Nemirovsky

Andee Rubin

Susan Jo Russell

Cornelia Tierney

Contributing Authors

Mary Berle-Carman

Rebecca B. Corwin

Rebeka Eston

Claryce Evans

Anne Goodrow

Cliff Konold

Chris Mainhart

Sue McMillen

Jerrie Moffet

Tracy Noble

Kim O'Neil

Mark Ogonowski

Julie Sarama

Amy Shulman Weinberg

Margie Singer

Virginia Woolley

Tracey Wright

Contents

UNIT 9

Penny Jars and Plant Growth

Investigations

Overview of Program Components

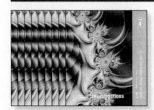

FOR TEACHERS

The **Curriculum Units** are the teaching guides. (See far right.)

Implementing Investigations in Grade 4 offers suggestions for implementing the curriculum. It also contains a comprehensive index.

The **Differentiation and Intervention Guide** offers additional activities for each Investigation to support the range of learners.

Investigations for the Interactive Whiteboard provides whole-class instructional support to enhance each session.

The **Resource Masters and Transparencies CD** contains all reproducible materials that support instruction. The **LogoPaths CD** provides an environment in which students investigate a variety of geometric ideas.

FOR STUDENTS

The **Student Activity Book** contains the consumable student pages (Recording Sheets, Homework, Practice, and so on).

The **Student Math Handbook** contains Math Words and Ideas pages and Games directions.

The *Investigations* Curriculum

Investigations in Number, Data, and Space® is a K–5 mathematics curriculum designed to engage students in making sense of mathematical ideas. Six major goals guided the development of the *Investigations in Number, Data, and Space*® curriculum. The curriculum is designed to:

- Support students to make sense of mathematics and learn that they can be mathematical thinkers

- Focus on computational fluency with whole numbers as a major goal of the elementary grades

- Provide substantive work in important areas of mathematics—rational numbers, geometry, measurement, data, and early algebra—and connections among them

- Emphasize reasoning about mathematical ideas

- Communicate mathematics content and pedagogy to teachers

- Engage the range of learners in understanding mathematics

Underlying these goals are three guiding principles that are touchstones for the *Investigations* team as we approach both students and teachers as agents of their own learning:

1. *Students have mathematical ideas.* Students come to school with ideas about numbers, shapes, measurements, patterns, and data. If given the opportunity to learn in an environment that stresses making sense of mathematics, students build on the ideas they already have and learn about new mathematics they have never encountered. Students learn that they are capable of having mathematical ideas, applying what they know to new situations, and thinking and reasoning about unfamiliar problems.

2. *Teachers are engaged in ongoing learning* about mathematics content, pedagogy, and student learning. The curriculum provides material for professional development, to be used by teachers individually or in groups, that supports teachers' continued learning as they use the curriculum over several years. The *Investigations* curriculum materials are designed as much to be a dialogue with teachers as to be a core of content for students.

3. *Teachers collaborate with the students and curriculum materials* to create the curriculum as enacted in the classroom. The only way for a good curriculum to be used well is for teachers to be active participants in implementing it. Teachers use the curriculum to maintain a clear, focused, and coherent agenda for mathematics teaching. At the same time, they observe and listen carefully to students, try to understand how they are thinking, and make teaching decisions based on these observations.

Investigations is based on experience from research and practice, including field testing that involved documentation of thousands of hours in classrooms, observations of students, input from teachers, and analysis of student work. As a result, the curriculum addresses the learning needs of real students in a wide range of classrooms and communities. The investigations are carefully designed to invite all students into mathematics—girls and boys; members of diverse cultural, ethnic, and language groups; and students with a wide variety of strengths, needs, and interests.

Based on this extensive classroom testing, the curriculum takes seriously the time students need to develop a strong conceptual foundation and skills based on that foundation. Each curriculum unit focuses on an area of content in depth, providing time for students to develop and practice ideas across a variety of activities and contexts that build on each other. Daily guidelines for time spent on class sessions, Classroom Routines (K–3), and Ten-Minute Math (3–5) reflect the commitment to devoting adequate time to mathematics in each school day.

About This Curriculum Unit

This **Curriculum Unit** is one of nine teaching guides in Grade 4. The ninth unit in Grade 4 is *Penny Jars and Plant Growth.*

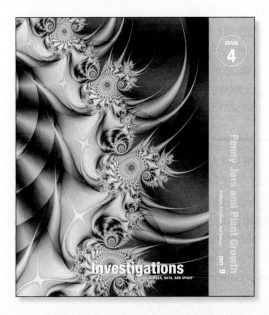

- The **Introduction and Overview** section organizes and presents the instructional materials, provides background information, and highlights important features specific to this unit.

- Each Curriculum Unit contains several **Investigations.** Each Investigation focuses on a set of related mathematical ideas.

- Investigations are divided into one-hour **Sessions,** or lessons.

- Sessions have a combination of these parts: **Activity, Discussion, Math Workshop, Assessment Activity,** and **Session Follow-Up.**

- Each session also has one or more **Ten-Minute Math** activities that are done outside of math time.

- At the back of the book is a collection of **Teacher Notes** and **Dialogue Boxes** that provide professional development related to the unit.

- Also included at the back of the book are the **Student Math Handbook** pages for this unit.

- The **Index** provides a way to look up important words or terms.

Overview

O F   T H I S   U N I T

Investigation	Session	Day	
INVESTIGATION 1 **Looking at Graphs** Students examine graphs of temperature and speed. They determine values of the points on the graphs, identify changes in temperature or speed, and relate the changes that are represented on the graphs to the corresponding stories.	**1.1** Temperature and Speed	1	
	1.2 The Marathon	2	
INVESTIGATION 2 **Penny Jars and Towers** Students work with situations of constant change to examine and make predictions about how values change. They use tables, graphs, arithmetic expressions, and symbolic notation to represent, describe, and compare situations of constant change.	**2.1** The Penny Jar	3	
	2.2 Penny Jar Tables	4	
	2.3 Round 20	5	
	2.4 Penny Jar Graphs	6	
	2.5 Assessment: Penny Jar Comparisons	7	
	2.6 Can There Be 15 Windows?	8	
	2.7 Comparing Penny Jar Situations	9	
	2.8 Rules for Windows and Towers	10	
INVESTIGATION 3 **Collecting and Analyzing Measurements** Students make line graphs of plant growth, describe the change in growth that graphs represent, and match graphs with tables and stories.	**3.1** Graphing and Predicting Plant Growth	11	
	3.2 Using Line Graphs to Compare Growth	12	
	3.3 Graphs, Stories, and Tables	13	
	3.4 Straight or Not? Increasing or Decreasing?	14	
	3.5 End-of-Unit Assessment	15	

Each *Investigations* session has some combination of these five parts: **Activity, Discussion, Math Workshop, Assessment Activity,** and **Session Follow-Up.** These session parts are indicated in the chart below. Each session also has one **Ten-Minute Math** activity that is done outside of math time.

 Ⓦ Interactive Whiteboard

Ten-Minute Math

Activity	Discussion	Math Workshop	Assessment Activity	Session Follow-Up
Ⓦ Ⓦ	Ⓦ			●
Ⓦ	Ⓦ ●			●
Ⓦ ●	Ⓦ			●
Ⓦ	Ⓦ			●
Ⓦ	Ⓦ			●
●	Ⓦ Ⓦ			●
Ⓦ		●		●
	Ⓦ	●		●
	Ⓦ	●		●
Ⓦ	Ⓦ			●
Ⓦ ●	Ⓦ			●
●	●			●
Ⓦ	Ⓦ			●
●	Ⓦ			●
			●	●

Quick Survey	Closest Estimate
Ⓦ	
Ⓦ	
	Ⓦ
	Ⓦ
Ⓦ	
	Ⓦ
	Ⓦ
	Ⓦ
Ⓦ	
	Ⓦ
Ⓦ	
Ⓦ	
	Ⓦ
	Ⓦ
Ⓦ	

Mathematics

IN THIS UNIT

Penny Jars and Plant Growth is the Grade 4 unit in the Patterns, Functions and Change strand of *Investigations*. These units develop ideas about patterns, sequences, and functions and are part of the early algebra foundation integrated into the *Investigations* curriculum.

In Grade 3, students graphed the temperature throughout the school year and described graphs of temperature in several international sites. Through discussing these line graphs, they learned how this kind of graph represents change over time. Students in Grade 3 usually begin the year describing each individual change ("it went up, then down, then down again, then up"), but end the year describing trends ("the temperature gradually kept going down from September to December"). As they worked with line graphs, they also learned about the conventions of this kind of graph —in particular, how a point on the graph represents a correspondence between two values (e.g., in temperature graphs, time is measured along the *x*-axis and temperature is measured along the *y*-axis).

Students also worked with situations with a rate of change in the context of repeating color patterns and the context of children who receive a certain number of "magic marbles" each day. Building on their work with tables in Grade 2, students continued to use tables and added graphs to their repertoire of representations. They also articulated rules that describe the relationship between two variables in a situation with a constant rate of change. In doing so, they considered two kinds of quantities: a starting amount and a constant amount of change. For example: *I start with 30 marbles in my marble collection; I add 3 marbles each day.* Their work focused on connecting the situation, the table, the graph, and the rule. They also used tables and graphs to compare different situations of constant change. For example: *Franick starts with 30 marbles and gets 3 each day while Bolar starts with no marbles and gets 5 each day. Will Bolar ever have as many marbles as Franick?*

This unit focuses on 3 Mathematical Emphases:

1 Using Tables and Graphs **Using graphs to represent change**

Math Focus Points

- Interpreting the points and shape of a graph in terms of the situation the graph represents

- Finding the difference between two values on a line graph

- Discriminating between features of a graph that represent quantity and those that represent changes in quantity

- Identifying points in a graph with corresponding values in a table and interpreting the numerical information in terms of the situation the graph represents

- Plotting points on a coordinate grid to represent a situation in which one quantity is changing in relation to another

- Comparing situations by describing the differences in their graphs

- Describing the relative steepness of graphs or parts of graphs in terms of different rates of change

- Comparing tables, graphs, and situations of constant change with those of non-constant change

Line graphs are used to show a correspondence between two quantities. For values on the horizontal axis, or *x*-axis, there are corresponding values measured along the vertical axis, or *y*-axis. Points placed on a coordinate grid show this correspondence. For example, as students graph the growth of their plants in Investigation 3, each point on their graphs shows a particular time and a corresponding value for height. Students can see that the height is increasing, but they can also describe and compare the rate of that increase over different periods of time shown on the graph.

An emphasis in this unit is on how a line graph shows the *rate of change.* In Investigation 1, students consider the difference between parts of a story that are about speed as well as parts of a story that are about *changes in speed,* and the way the graph shows each of these.

In Investigation 3, when students describe graphs of plant growth, they consider not only specific heights, but also the rate of growth of the plant: when was it growing more slowly or more quickly?

Students also create graphs for situations in which the rate of change is constant. Both the Penny Jar context and the Windows and Towers context in Investigation 2 are such situations. In contrast to the graphs in Investigations 1 and 3, the points on a graph for one of these situations fall in a straight line; they have a constant *slope.* Although students do not use the word "slope," they do talk about the relative steepness of lines representing different situations of constant change. For example, Penny Jar A has 8 pennies in the jar at first and 2 pennies are added in each round; Penny Jar B has 0 pennies in the jar at first and 4 pennies are added in each round. The graph for Penny Jar B starts lower on the *y*-axis, but it slants more steeply and soon crosses and passes Penny Jar A.

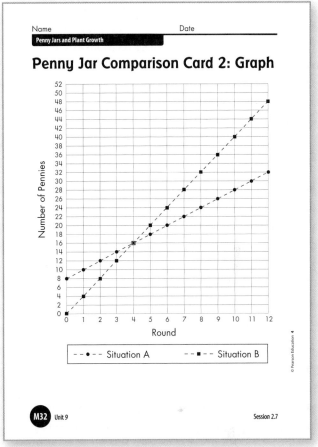

▲ Resource Masters, M32

2 Using Tables and Graphs: **Using tables to represent change**

Math Focus Points

◆ Using tables to represent the relationship between two quantities in a situation of constant change

◆ Interpreting numbers in a table in terms of the situation they represent

Tables are another form of representation that shows how one quantity changes in relation to another. Organizing data in a table and examining the relationship between columns of the table is one way to uncover a rule that governs that relationship. Students come into Grade 4 with a great deal of experience with tables. However, they need to look carefully at how the entries in a table are listed: is every entry listed sequentially, or are there jumps or gaps in the entries?

The number patterns that students see in a column of a table can be particularly compelling. If students see a column in which the numbers are 8, 10, 12, 14, it is easy for them to simply continue the pattern—counting by 2s—without thinking about how these numbers represent the situation. See **Dialogue Box:** "I took a guess that there was a pattern," page 154.

Throughout their work, students move between tables and graphs and between these representations and the situations they represent. By looking at how features of the situation are represented in the table or graph and how features of a table appear in a graph and vice versa, students learn a great deal about mathematical relationships.

3 Linear Change Describing and representing a constant rate of change

Math Focus Points

- Finding the value of one quantity in a situation of constant change, given the value of the other

- Creating a representation for a situation of constant change

- Describing the relationship between two quantities in a situation of constant change, taking into account a beginning amount and a constant increase

- Writing an arithmetic expression for finding the value of one quantity in terms of the other in a situation of constant change

- Making rules that relate one variable to another in situations of constant change

- Using symbolic letter notation to represent the value of one variable in terms of another

In Investigation 2, students work with two contexts that involve a constant rate of change—Penny Jars and Windows and Towers. See **Teacher Note:** Situations with a Constant Rate of Change: Linear Functions, page 138. They have described and represented such situations—which are linear functions—in earlier grades. They noticed that in such situations, there is a starting amount (which may be 0) and a constant rate of change. In this unit, they delve more deeply into how these two aspects of the function define the relationship between the two quantities by considering questions such as "Can you find the number of pennies in the jar after Round 10 by doubling the number of pennies in the jar after Round 5?" See **Dialogue Box:** Doubling or Not?, page 156.

This work leads students to articulate a general rule for the situation so that if the value of one variable (the Round number) is known, the corresponding value of the other variable (number of pennies in the jar) can be calculated. At first students articulate these rules in words (as they did in Grade 3), but they also are introduced to the use of symbolic notation and equations to represent their rules.

This Unit also focuses on

- Measuring in centimeters

Ten-Minute Math activities focus on

- Describing features of the data

- Interpreting and posing questions about the data

- Approximating numbers to nearby landmark numbers, e.g., multiples of 10 or 100

- Calculating mentally

- Comparing answer choices to find the one closest to the actual answer

LOOKING FORWARD

In Grade 5, students continue to work on describing and representing linear functions in new contexts. They develop rules to describe the relationship between quantities in these situations and gain more experience in using symbolic notation to express these rules as equations. They also encounter situations in which the change is not constant, but the rate of change itself changes in a predictable way. For example, as students consider the area of squares built with tiles, they find that when they graph the area of the square against the side length, the graph is not a straight line. The area increases faster and faster as the side of the square increases by 1.

Technology Note

Using the *LogoPaths* Software If you are using the *LogoPaths* software this year, give students ongoing access to the computers **outside of math time** during this unit. *LogoPaths* Resource Masters (M1–M6) offer continued work with *Missing Measures* and *Steps* activities. Students can also continue to play *Mazes* and spend time working with the *Free Explore* option of the software. See **Part 5: Technology** in *Investigations: Calculators and Computers* in *Implementing Investigations in Grade 4: Introducing and Managing the LogoPaths* software in Grade 4.

Unit Preparation for Investigation 3

Note: Preparation for the study of growing plants must begin as soon as you begin Investigation 1 of this unit. This will allow time for the plants to grow so that students will all have measurements to work with in Investigation 3.

Materials

- Lima bean seeds or dried lima beans for planting (3 per pair, plus extras)

- Paper towels (2 per pair)

- Transparent plastic cups or jars (1 per pair)

- Plastic wrap, enough to cover each cup

- Elastic bands (1 per pair)

- Marking pens

- Labels or masking tape for marking plant containers

- Plant pots (peat-moss pots work well) or small milk cartons (1 per student)

- Potting soil (about 5 pounds)

- Plant fertilizer (optional)

- Centimeter rulers (1 per pair)

- Sticks and string or twist ties for holding plants straight (optional)

- *Student Activity Book* pages 1–2

1. Soaking the Beans Overnight

When: When you start this unit (i.e., the night before Investigation 1, Session 1 or perhaps a day earlier or later)

Directions: Put seeds in a cup or bowl and cover them with water. Allow them to soak overnight.

2. Sprouting the Seeds

When: The day after the night you soak the seeds

Time: You will need approximately 30 minutes to have a brief discussion with your students and prepare the seeds for sprouting.

Directions: Show students the seeds that have been soaking. Explain that they will be taking care of some seeds, first sprouting them and then planting them in order to discover how they change over time. Ask students to share their ideas about how the plants will change.

What do you think will happen first? After that? How much do you think the plants will grow each day? Do you think that the plants will grow the same or a different amount each day? Do you think they will grow faster when they first start growing or after a week or two?

Students will probably have different ideas about the answers to these questions. Allow them to share their ideas without commenting on their correctness at this time.

Demonstrate the following steps. Students who are absent for this session may use the seeds you prepare.

- Wet two paper towels and wring out the excess water.

- Fold the paper towels into a strip about as wide as the height of the cup, and curve it around the inside of the cup.

- Place the seeds between the cup and the paper towel so that the paper towel holds them in place.

- Add water to touch the paper towel but not cover the seeds.

- Put plastic wrap over the top of the cup to limit evaporation. Fasten with an elastic band.

- Label the container with the appropriate student names and put it in a dark place until the seeds sprout.

Pairs of students select three of the soaked seeds and follow the procedure you demonstrated. Establish a prescribed time, approximately the same time each day, for students to check their seeds and to add water if necessary. If a seed becomes moldy, students should remove it and change the paper towel. Remind students to keep the water level so that it touches the towel but does not cover the seeds. This monitoring does not need to be a part of the mathematics class, but it must not be forgotten.

Tell students that after a few days, when roots appear on the seeds, they will plant the seeds in dirt. When most students' seeds have roots, proceed to Part 3.

3. Planting the Seeds

When: When most of the sprouting seeds have roots (usually a few days after Part 2)

Time: You will need approximately 30 minutes for students to plant their seeds in soil.

Directions: Working with their partners, students choose two healthy seeds that have roots. If they are using milk cartons as planting pots, be sure that they put a small drainage hole in the bottom. For each seed, they fill a pot almost to the top with soil and soak the soil with water. Then, with a finger, they make a hole in the soil deep enough to accommodate the seed. They gently place the sprouted seed, root down, in the hole. They pack the soil around the seed loosely and put a shallow layer of soil over it. Finally, they label the plant pots with their names and perhaps a number or letter for each plant.

The soil should be allowed to dry out between waterings and should be kept in a warm area, near a brightly lit window, if possible. Continue to have students tend plants daily.

It is recommended that students work in pairs with only one plant. They can begin by keeping both planted seeds until one germinates. They keep the plant that sprouts first and take daily measurements of its height. They put aside the other planted seed, or if it has also germinated, they can give it to a pair of students who have no germinated plant. Collect a few of the extra planted seeds to care for in case something happens to some students' plants. You will need to keep track of the heights of these plants after they sprout so that you can pass on the information to students who assume their care.

Once the stems of the plants start to grow, your students may want to add plant fertilizer to the water. After four to six days, when some of the stems have grown to about 1 centimeter, students will start to keep track of their plants' changing heights. At that point, continue to Part 4.

4. Measuring the Plants

When: As soon as the stem of at least one bean plant is visible

Time: On the first day of measuring, you will need approximately 30 minutes to work with students to make and record their first measurement. Then students need a few minutes each day to measure their plants and record their measurements.

Directions: As soon as the stem of one or more students' plants is visible, have students turn to *Student Activity Book* pages 1–2. Although student pairs will share plants, each student will keep his or her own recording chart. All students begin collecting data at this point. Those whose plants have no visible growth will write 0 cm on their charts.

Use one of the plants whose stem has been growing to demonstrate how to measure. Place a centimeter ruler on the top of the soil. Some rulers have a little extra space at the end before the zero point; in this case, remind students to poke the end of the ruler into the dirt so that the zero mark is just at the surface. Measure to the top of the stem, to the nearest half centimeter, and point out where this measurement should be recorded on the *Student Activity Book* page. Tell your students to measure as carefully as possible to the nearest half centimeter.

Students should also be careful to keep the soil around the base of the stem level. If the stem starts to lean to one side, they should gently straighten it before taking their measurements.

Help students establish the routine of recording heights daily, initially just on their charts. Later, in Investigation 3, Line Graphs and Plant Growth, they will record heights on their graphs as well.

Assessment

IN THIS UNIT

ONGOING ASSESSMENT: Observing Students at Work

The following sessions provide **Ongoing Assessment: Observing Students at Work** opportunities:

- **Session 1.1, pp. 28 and 32**
- **Session 1.2, p. 37**
- **Session 2.1, pp. 48 and 49**
- **Session 2.2, pp. 56–57**
- **Session 2.3, p. 63**
- **Session 2.4, p. 71**
- **Session 2.5, pp. 80–81 and 83**
- **Session 2.6, pp. 87, 88, and 89**
- **Session 2.8, p. 100**
- **Session 3.1, pp. 109 and 112**
- **Session 3.2, p. 116**
- **Session 3.3, p. 121**
- **Session 3.4, p. 128**
- **Session 3.5, p. 131**

WRITING OPPORTUNITIES

The following sessions have **writing** opportunities for students to explain their mathematical thinking:

- **Session 1.1, p. 32**
  Student Activity Book, p. 6
- **Session 2.1, p. 53**
  Student Activity Book, p. 15
- **Session 2.2, p. 55**
  Student Activity Book, p. 18
- **Session 2.3, pp. 62–63**
  Student Activity Book, pp. 21–22
- **Session 2.5, p. 81**
  Student Activity Book, pp. 35 and 37

PORTFOLIO OPPORTUNITIES

The following sessions have work appropriate for a **portfolio:**

- **Session 2.3, pp. 62–63**
  Student Activity Book, pp. 21–22
- **Session 2.5, pp. 81–82**
  Student Activity Book, pp. 35–37
  Penny Jar Comparisons, M28–M30
- **Session 3.1, pp. 108 and 112**
  Students' graphs of their plants' growth and *Student Activity Book,* p. 60
- **Session 3.5, pp. 130–131**
  M37–M39, End-of-Unit Assessment

Assessing the Benchmarks

Observing students as they engage in conversation about their ideas is a primary means to assess their mathematical understanding. Consider all of your students' work, not just the written assessments. See the chart below for suggestions about key activities to observe.

See the **Differentiation and Intervention Guide** for quizzes that can be used after each Investigation.

Benchmarks in This Unit	Key Activities to Observe	Assessment
1. Connect tables and graphs to each other and to the situations they represent.	**Session 1.2:** Making a Speed Graph **Session 2.4:** Matching Tables and Graphs **Session 3.3:** Matching Numbers, Stories, and Graphs	**Session 2.5:** Assessment: Penny Jar Comparisons ✓ **Session 3.5 End-of-Unit Assessment:** Problems 2, 3, and 4
2. Make a graph on a coordinate grid from a table of values.	**Session 2.4:** Making Graphs	**Session 2.5:** Assessment: Penny Jar Comparisons
3. Describe how a graph shows change: where the rate of change is increasing, decreasing, or remaining constant, and how differences in steepness represent differences in the rate of change.	**Session 1.2:** Making a Speed Graph **Session 2.5:** Assessment: Penny Jar Comparisons **Session 3.2:** Comparing Growth of Different Plants	**Session 3.5 End-of-Unit Assessment:** Problems 1, 2, and 3
4. Take into account the starting amount and the amount of change in describing and comparing situations of constant change.	**Session 2.5:** Assessment: Penny Jar Comparisons	**Session 2.5:** Assessment: Penny Jar Comparisons **Session 3.5 End-of-Unit Assessment:** Problem 5
5. In a situation of constant change, write rules (using words or arithmetic expressions) to determine the value of one quantity, given the value of the other.	**Session 2.8:** Rules for Towers	**Session 3.5 End-of-Unit Assessment:** Problem 5

 Checklist Available

Relating the Mathematical Emphases to the Benchmarks

Mathematical Emphases	Benchmarks
Using Tables and Graphs Using graphs to represent change	1, 2, and 3
Using Tables and Graphs Using tables to represent change	1
Linear Change Describing and representing a constant rate of change	1, 4, and 5

This essay is intended to illustrate how your students' ideas in this unit lay the foundation for algebra. While students in previous grades have been working with linear functions and articulating rules that relate two quantities, students are introduced to algebraic notation for the first time in Grade 4. This notation is introduced in a way that keeps it closely connected to a context with which students are working. By moving among the context, their own ways of describing general rules in words, and symbolic notation, students learn how this notation can carry mathematical meaning.

Consider the following vignette from a class working on Session 2.8 of this unit:

In this fourth-grade class, students are comparing the rules they have made for the number of windows on a "double tower" of cubes.

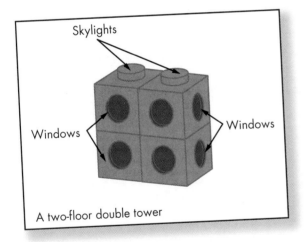

A two-floor double tower

Alejandro's group has written, "Floors × 6 + 2." The teacher asks the students to explain why this rule works by referring to the cube tower.

Ursula: Because there are two on the front, two on the back, and one on that side and that side. [She points to one floor of the tower and shows where all the windows are on that floor.]

Ursula uses the everyday language of "sides" of a building to refer to the faces of the cube tower.

Venetta: As many times as there are sides, is how many sides there are.

Teacher: OK, how many sides there are. I hear the word "sides" being used in a lot of ways. Venetta, can you clarify what you mean, and why you think Alejandro is saying "number of floors multiplied by 6" to get the number of windows?

Venetta: Well, you have to count the windows on one side of the building and then multiply it by the number or add that number—how many sides there are—that many times. Like on this one . . .

Teacher: Come up and show us.

Venetta: OK. Like on this one. [She picks up a double tower with 10 floors.] There are six sides: 1, 2, 3, 4, 5, 6 [she runs her finger down each column of cube faces]. There are 10 on each side, so add 10 six times. Ten plus 10 plus 10 plus 10 plus 10 plus 10, and then you have to add 2 skylights.

Teacher: Let's say this tower isn't 10 floors high anymore. I've just got this enormous building, and I know it's a certain number of floors. Would your rule still work for this enormous number?

Steve: Yes, you just do like that number times 6 because there's 6 windows, and it's that number for every floor.

Lucy: And add the 2 for the skylights.

In articulating their rule as "floors × 6 + 2," Alejandro's group has written something that approaches symbolic notation. This group has moved from describing relationships between quantities in sentences—for example, "take the number of floors and multiply that times 6 and then add 2 more for the skylights"—to shorthand, using words and numbers. "Floors," meaning the number of floors, is the variable that stands for *any number* of floors. In the discussion, this sense of "any number" is apparent in the students' words. Although there is a particular double tower with 10 floors that the students are handling, students repeatedly refer to a general "number." Venetta demonstrates why the rule works for the tower with 10 floors. Then Steve says, "Yes, you just do like *that number* times 6 because there's 6 windows, and it's *that number* for every floor."

Moving from "floors × 6 + 2" to $6 × F + 2$ is a small step when students are keeping in mind the meaning of the numbers and letters. In fact, this class has already been introduced to symbolic notation in Session 4. Some students are using equations such as $w = 6 × f + 2$, while others are using a combination of words and symbols, as Alejandro does.

In more conventional notation, this equation could be written as $y = 6x + 2$ where y (the dependent variable) represents the number of windows, and x (the independent variable) represents the number of floors. The two numbers in this equation—6 and 2—have very different interpretations. The 6 represents the *slope* or the rate of change. In this situation, 6 is the number of windows added to the total each time the number of floors increases by 1. The 2 represents a starting amount that is not affected by the value of the independent variable (the number of floors). In the double tower, this 2 represents the skylights—there are only 2 skylights no matter how many floors are in the tower. If we imagine a tower with 0 floors (a mathematical abstraction that helps us see the different parts of this equation), we can imagine the two skylights lying there, waiting for the rest of the building to be built! In this situation, when x (the number of floors) has a value of 0, y (the number of windows) = 2. On a graph of this equation, the point (0, 2) is where the graph intersects the y-axis. For this reason, this value is called the *y-intercept*.

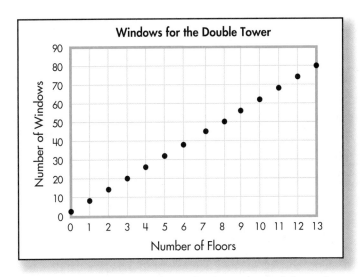

Windows for the Double Tower

Number of Windows (y-axis), *Number of Floors* (x-axis)

In this unit, students work on thinking through how the starting amount and the rate of change affect the behavior of the function. When they compare two Penny Jars, they consider whether a Penny Jar that starts out with fewer pennies will eventually "catch up" to a Penny Jar that starts out with more pennies. They notice that when the rate of change for two Penny Jars with different starting amounts is the same, their graphs never intersect. They always differ by the starting amount. They also notice that if one Penny Jar has a greater rate of change but a smaller starting amount than another, the first one will eventually have more pennies and their graphs will intersect.

For most adults, notation (the use of variables, operations, and equal signs) is the chief identifying feature of algebra. The notation expresses, in equations, rules that are satisfied by particular pairs of quantities. In later years, students learn to manipulate these equations in the abstract, disconnected from particular physical situations. Students' grounding in concrete contexts in the elementary grades supports their understanding of an equation such as the general linear form $y = mx + b$. It also prepares them to understand how changes in the values represented by these symbols affect the mathematical relationships represented by the equation. Students' *reasoning* about the mathematical relationship, *not* the notation, is the central work of elementary students in algebra.

Ten-Minute Math

Ten-Minute Math offers practice and review of key concepts for this grade level. These daily activities, to be done in ten minutes outside of math class, are introduced in a unit and repeated throughout the grade. Specific directions for the day's activity are provided in each session. For the full description and variations of each classroom activity, see *Implementing Investigations in Grade 4*.

Activity	Introduced	Full Description of Activity and Its Variations
Quick Survey	Unit 2, Session 1.1	*Implementing Investigations in Grade 4*
Closest Estimate	Unit 8, Session 1.1	*Implementing Investigations in Grade 4*

Quick Survey

Students collect, display, describe, and interpret data about themselves or something they can observe easily. Students describe what they can tell from the data, generate some new questions, and, if appropriate, make predictions about what will happen the next time they collect the same data.

Math Focus Points

- Describing features of the data

- Interpreting and posing questions about the data

Closest Estimate

Students choose the closest estimate for a given multiplication or division problem by computing mentally. They discuss their strategies for finding the estimate, including changing numbers to a landmark and breaking numbers apart for easier computation.

Math Focus Points

- Approximating numbers to nearby landmark numbers, e.g., multiples of 10 or 100

- Calculating mentally

- Comparing answer choices to find the one closest to the actual answer

Practice and Review

Practice and review play a critical role in the *Investigations* program. The following components and features are available to provide regular reinforcement of key mathematical concepts and procedures.

Books	Features	In This Unit . . .
Curriculum Unit	**Ten-Minute Math** offers practice and review of key concepts for this grade level. These daily activities, to be done in ten minutes outside of math class, are introduced in a unit and repeated throughout the grade. Specific directions for the day's activity are provided in each session. For the full description and variations of each classroom activity, see *Implementing Investigations in Grade 4*.	• **All sessions**
Student Activity Book	**Daily Practice** pages in the *Student Activity Book* provide one of three types of written practice: **reinforcement** of the content of the unit, **ongoing review,** or **enrichment** opportunities. Some Daily Practice pages will also have Ongoing Review items with multiple-choice problems similar to those on standardized tests.	• **All sessions**
	Homework pages in the *Student Activity Book* are an extension of the work done in class. At times they help students prepare for upcoming activities.	• **Sessions 1.1, 1.2, 2.1, 2.2, 2.3, 2.4, 2.5, 2.6, 2.7, 2.8, 3.1, 3.2, 3.3, 3.4**
Student Math Handbook	**Math Words and Ideas** in the *Student Math Handbook* are pages that summarize key words and ideas. Most Words and Ideas pages have at least one exercise.	• **Student Math Handbook, pp. 72–86**
	Games pages are found in a section of the *Student Math Handbook*.	• **No games are introduced in this unit.**

Supporting the Range of Learners

The **Differentiation and Intervention Guide** provides Intervention, Extension, and Practice activities for use within each Investigation.

Sessions	1.1	1.2	2.1	2.2	2.3	2.4	2.5	2.6	2.8	3.1	3.2	3.3	3.4
Intervention	•	•	•	•	•	•	•	•	•	•	•	•	•
Extension	•		•	•	•	•	•	•	•				•
ELL		•	•							•		•	

Intervention

Suggestions are made to support and engage students who are having difficulty with a particular idea, activity, or problem.

Extension

Suggestions are made to support and engage students who finish early or may be ready for an additional challenge.

English Language Learners (ELL)

As English Language Learners work through the material in *Penny Jars and Plant Growth,* some may need additional support with the language used to describe line graphs and the differences among various graphs, including terms such as *straight line, diagonal, highest point, lowest point, gradual slope, steep slope, jagged.* Whenever possible, point to a visual example as these terms come up in discussion. Encourage all students to use hand and arm gestures as they describe the different types of line. For additional support, remind students to refer to the Math Words and Ideas pages about line graphs in the *Student Math Handbook.*

Preview vocabulary that will be used throughout the Windows and Towers activities, starting in Session 2.5. Have photographs of tall buildings with distinct, countable windows to help English Language Learners understand the metaphorical relationship to the cube towers in the activity. Relate each additional layer of cubes to another

"floor" on the building. Also clarify the interchangeable use of *stories* and *floors:* A building that is 10 *stories* high has 10 *floors.*

Make sure students understand that the round holes on the faces of the cubes represent *windows,* and the knob on top of the cube represents a *skylight,* or a window that faces up toward the sky. Be sure they recognize the names for *single, double, square,* and *corner* towers and can apply them to the towers illustrated in Sessions 2.5 and 2.6.

Working with the Range of Learners: Classroom Cases is a set of episodes written by teachers that focuses on meeting the needs of the range of learners in the classroom. In the first section, *Setting up the Mathematical Community,* teachers write about how they create a supportive and productive learning environment in their classrooms. In the next section, *Accommodations for Learning,* teachers focus on specific modifications they make to meet the needs of some of their learners. In the last section, *Language and Representation,* teachers share how they help students use representations and develop language to investigate and express mathematical ideas. The questions at the end of each case provide a starting point for your own reflection or for discussion with colleagues. See *Implementing Investigations in Grade 4* for this set of episodes.

Mathematical Emphasis

Using Tables and Graphs Using graphs to represent change

Math Focus Points

◆ Interpreting the points and shape of a graph in terms of the situation the graph represents

◆ Finding the difference between two values on a line graph

◆ Discriminating between features of a graph that represent quantity and those that represent changes in quantity

Looking at Graphs

	Student Activity Book	Student Math Handbook	Professional Development: Read Ahead of Time	
SESSION 1.1 p. 26				
Temperature and Speed Students determine values of points on graphs of temperature and speed. They identify sections of the graph where temperature or speed is increasing, decreasing, and remaining constant.	3–7	72–76	• **Mathematics in This Unit,** p. 10 • **Algebra Connections in This Unit,** p. 18 • **Dialogue Box:** How Is The Temperature Changing?, p. 153 • **Teacher Note:** Using Line Graphs to Represent Change, p. 133 • **Part 4: Ten-Minute Math** in *Implementing Investigations in Grade 4: Quick Survey*	
SESSION 1.2 p. 34				
The Marathon Students identify phrases about speed and changes in speed in a story, and make a graph that corresponds to the story.	5–6, 8–12	75–76		

Materials to Gather	Materials to Prepare
• **T86, Temperatures in Two Cities** 🖨 • **T87, The Motion Graph** 🖨	• **Note:** Be sure to begin the Unit Preparation activity on pages 13–15 with your students. It lays crucial groundwork for Investigation 3 in this unit. • **M9–M10, Family Letter** Make copies. (1 per student)
• **T87, The Motion Graph** (from Session 1.1) 🖨 • **T88–T89, The Boston Marathon** 🖨 • **Tape**	• **M13–M14, Family Letter** Make copies. (1 per student)

🖨 Overhead Transparency

Temperature and Speed

Math Focus Points

◈ Interpreting the points and shape of a graph in terms of the situation the graph represents

◈ Finding the difference between two values on a line graph

Vocabulary

graph

axis

Today's Plan			Materials
1 ACTIVITY **Examining Temperature Graphs**	20 MIN	PAIRS	• *Student Activity Book,* pp. 3–4 • T86
2 DISCUSSION **Temperature Graphs**	20 MIN	CLASS	• *Student Activity Book,* pp. 3–4 • T86
3 ACTIVITY **Reading Speed Graphs**	20 MIN	PAIRS	• *Student Activity Book,* pp. 5–6 • T87
4 SESSION FOLLOW-UP **Daily Practice and Homework**			• *Student Activity Book,* pp. 5–7 • *Student Math Handbook,* pp. 72–76 • M9–M10, Family Letter*

*See *Materials to Prepare,* p. 25.

Ten-Minute Math

Quick Survey For the survey, ask the class, "What did you eat for breakfast this morning?" or a different categorical question that you or the students choose. Make sure they collect data about something they already know or can observe easily and that is likely to change on a different day. Keep the class data to use for comparison in the next session. With today's data, make a bar graph. Ask students:

• What do you notice about the data?

• What do the data tell us about our class?

ACTIVITY

Examining Temperature Graphs

This new unit in mathematics focuses on making and using **graphs** and tables to describe how things change—such as temperature, penny jars, cube buildings, and plant growth.❶

In this session, students review how to read and interpret graphs on a coordinate grid showing change over time. Have students turn to *Student Activity Book* pages 3–4. You may want to locate Moscow and Sydney on a world map. Some students may remember similar work about temperature from Grade 3 in the unit *Stories, Tables, and Graphs.*

What do you think the graph on page 3 is about?

Ask students to trace over the line graph for each city with a different-colored pencil or marker. This facilitates matching each city with its graph and also allows students to get a sense of the general shape of each graph.

Color-coding the lines on the graph aids student understanding.

Invite students to make general comments about what they see in the graphs.

What do you notice about the temperatures in Moscow and Sydney?

Teaching Note

❶ **Measuring Growth**   As you begin this unit, start the Unit Preparation activity (pages 13–15), growing lima bean plants. Students use *Student Activity Book* pages 1–2 to collect measurement data about the growth of their plants. They need these data for use in Investigation 3.

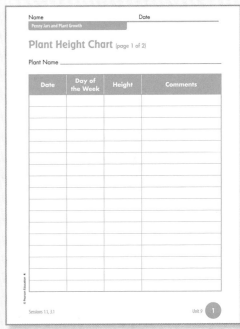

▲ **Student Activity Book, p. 1**

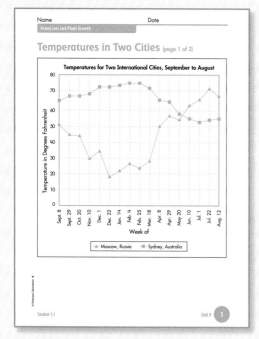

Plant Height Chart (page 2 of 2)

▲ Student Activity Book, p. 2

Temperatures in Two Cities (page 1 of 2)

▲ Student Activity Book, p. 3;
Transparencies, T86

Students might say:

"The highest temperature occurs in Sydney in February."

"Sydney has its highest temperature around the same time that Moscow has its lowest."

"The range of temperatures in Sydney is smaller than the range in Moscow."

As students offer comments, have them explain what they see on the graph. After three or four statements have been made and explained, have students work in pairs on *Student Activity Book* page 4.

If students in your class seem unfamiliar with the conventions of reading graphs like this one, spend a few minutes pointing to specific points on the graph. Use the transparency of Temperatures in Two Cities (T86), and ask students to explain the meaning of each point—for example, "That point means that on April 29, it was about 56 or 57 degrees in Moscow."

ONGOING ASSESSMENT: Observing Students at Work

Students answer questions about features of the two-city temperature graph.

- **Are students able to read the graph (i.e., for a given date and given city, can they determine the temperature)?**

- **Do students understand that a higher point on the graph indicates a higher temperature?**

- **Can students find the difference between the hottest and coldest temperatures?**

As you circulate, ask students what features of the graph (height, the way the graph rises or falls, etc.) they are using to answer the questions. Ask them to explain their method for finding the difference between the hottest and coldest temperatures for a given city.

DIFFERENTIATION: Supporting the Range of Learners

Intervention Students who do not have experience reading graphs and are having difficulty answering the questions can begin by making a table for one city to show the temperatures for each date. They can refer to *Student Math Handbook* to see data both in a table and on a graph.

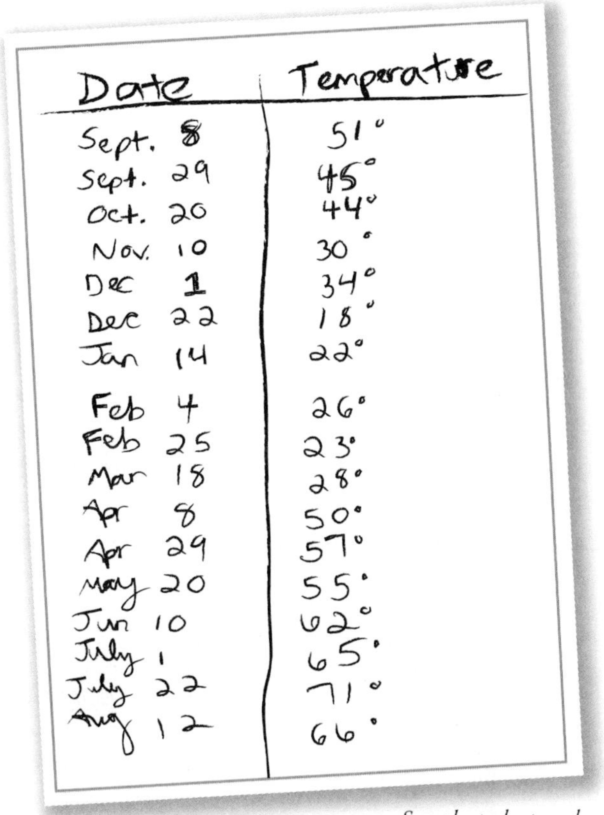

Date	Temperature
Sept. 8	51°
Sept. 29	45°
Oct. 20	44°
Nov. 10	30°
Dec 1	34°
Dec 22	18°
Jan 14	22°
Feb 4	26°
Feb 25	23°
Mar 18	28°
Apr 8	50°
Apr 29	57°
May 20	55°
Jun 10	62°
July 1	65°
July 22	71°
Aug 12	66°

Sample student work

Extension If some students finish early, pose these additional questions:

What is the difference between the highest temperature in Moscow and the highest temperature in Sydney? How much warmer is it in Sydney than in Moscow?

Name Date

Penny Jars and Plant Growth

Temperatures in Two Cities (page 2 of 2)

Look at the graph on the previous page to answer these questions:

1. Which place has the hottest temperature? ______
2. Which place has the coldest temperature? ______

Sydney:

3. During which week was it hottest? ______
4. What was the hottest temperature? ______
5. During which week was it coldest? ______
6. What was the coldest temperature? ______
7. What was the difference between Sydney's hottest and coldest temperatures? ______

Moscow:

8. During which week was it hottest? ______
9. What was the hottest temperature? ______
10. During which week was it coldest? ______
11. What was the coldest temperature? ______
12. What was the difference between Moscow's hottest and coldest temperatures? ______

© Pearson Education 4

4 Unit 9 Session 1.1

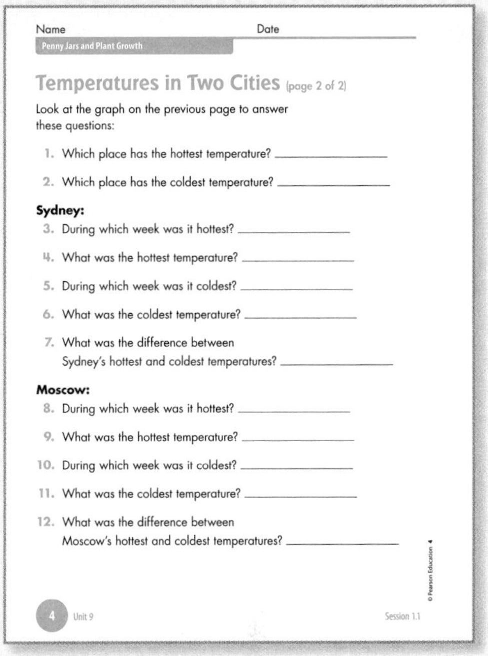

▲ **Student Activity Book, p. 4**

Professional Development

❷ **Dialogue Box:** How Is the Temperature Changing?, p. 153

Math Note

❸ **Estimation with Graphs** This graph does not have gridlines for each degree Fahrenheit. Stress to students that they may not be able to tell the exact temperature for some data points on their graph and that they will need to estimate instead. To help students estimate, ask questions such as "Is it hotter or colder than 50 degrees in Moscow on September 8th?" and "How can you tell?" Students' estimates may vary by one or two degrees.

DISCUSSION

❷ Temperature Graphs

20 MIN   CLASS

Math Focus Points for Discussion

◆ Interpreting the points and shape of a graph in terms of the situation the graph represents

◆ Finding the difference between two values on a line graph

Display the transparency of Temperatures in Two Cities (T86). Students can refer to the graph on *Student Activity Book* page 3.

What do you notice as you look at the whole graph of Moscow from September to August? What do you see happening over the whole year? How is that the same as or different from our temperature from September to August? What about the temperature in Sydney—how would you describe that?❷

Then focus the discussion on how students figured out the difference between the hottest and coldest temperatures in each city. Ask students to compare the hottest and coldest temperatures for each city and have them talk through any disagreements. Then invite two or three students to explain how they arrived at an answer.❸

Students explain how they found the difference between the hottest and coldest temperatures.

ACTIVITY

③ Reading Speed Graphs

20 MIN   PAIRS

In this activity, students examine a graph of speed. Have students turn to *Student Activity Book* pages 5–6. In these 20 minutes, orient students to this graph and help them get started by using the transparency of The Motion Graph (T87).

Before students begin their work in pairs, ask some general questions about this speed graph to connect with their work on temperature graphs. Help students understand the meaning of both axes—that the horizontal axis shows time and that the vertical axis shows speed.

In the graphs about temperature, when we moved from left to right on the graph, we were showing the change from September through August.

[Demonstrate by moving your finger along the motion graph on the transparency from left to right.]

This graph is about a runner in a race. What does it mean to move from left to right on this graph?

Explain to students that moving left to right means that time is going by. Make sure that they recognize that because the axes of the graph are not marked with values, it is unclear exactly how much time is passing—it could be a few minutes, an hour, or any other amount. This graph shows the overall shape of what is happening, but does not contain specific values.

In our graphs about temperature, a point higher up meant "warmer" and a point lower down meant "colder." This graph is about speed. What does a point up high mean? What does a point down low mean?

What if the runner stops? Would you say that the runner has a high speed or a low speed? If we say it is a low speed, is there a speed that is any lower? We can say that if the runner stops, the speed is zero. Where is this on the graph?

As students work in pairs, ask questions about the connections they are making between the shape of the graph and the speed of the runner.

How does the graph tell you that the runner is speeding up (or slowing down, or traveling steadily, or stopped)? ④ ⑤

Math Note

④ **Reading Graphs** In a graph of speed over time, many students at first perceive a horizontal line segment (which represents constant speed) as signifying no speed—or stopping. A horizontal line shows constant speed; that constant speed is zero only when the horizontal line is on the *x*-axis. Otherwise, a line segment such as segment *a*, *c*, or *g* shows that some speed greater than zero remains constant.

Professional Development

⑤ **Teacher Note:** Using Line Graphs to Represent Change, p. 133

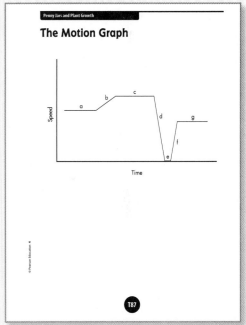

▲ Transparencies, T87

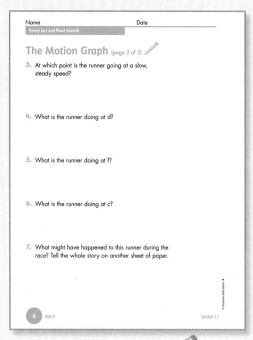

▲ **Student Activity Book, p. 5**

▲ **Student Activity Book, p. 6**

ONGOING ASSESSMENT: Observing Students at Work

Using the motion graph, students answer questions about what the different parts of the graph show.

- **Do students interpret level sections of the graph as steady speed?**

- **Do students interpret slanted sections of the graph as changes in speed?**

- **Do students interpret speed at zero as stopped?**

DIFFERENTIATION: Supporting the Range of Learners

Intervention The graph of speed will be less familiar to many students than the graph of temperature. Some students may find this graph difficult to interpret. If there are students who are ready to start, ask them to work in pairs.

Invite other students to meet with you in a small group. Help these students visualize increasing, decreasing, and constant speed by using a simple story in a context that is familiar to them. For example, tell a brief story about a subway train (or any mode of transportation familiar to your students) starting out from the station, increasing speed, then going at a constant speed, then slowing down as it reaches the next station, and then stopping for a minute while passengers get on and off.

With students, sketch how the speed changes and talk about how each piece of the graph should look:

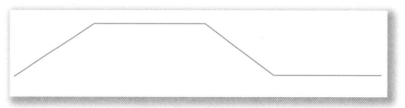

Some students may benefit from talking about numerical values for speed.

If the train starts at zero miles per hour and is going to increase its speed to 30 miles per hour, what will that part of the graph look like? Now it stays at 30 miles per hour for a few minutes. What will that part of the graph look like?

SESSION FOLLOW-UP

Daily Practice and Homework

 Daily Practice: For a reinforcement of this unit's content, have students complete *Student Activity Book* page 7.

 Homework: Students finish working on *Student Activity Book* pages 5–6.

 Student Math Handbook: Students and families may use *Student Math Handbook* pages 72–76 for reference and review. See pages 163–166 in the back of this unit.

 Family Letter: Send home copies of the Family Letter (M9–M10).

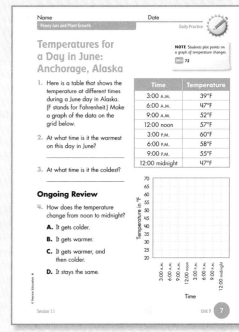

▲ **Student Activity Book, p. 7**

The Marathon

Math Focus Points

◆ Interpreting the points and shape of a graph in terms of the situation the graph represents

◆ Discriminating between features of a graph that represent quantity and those that represent changes in quantity

Today's Plan			Materials
DISCUSSION ❶ **The Motion Graph**	🕙 10 MIN	👥 CLASS	• *Student Activity Book*, pp. 5–6 (from Session 1.1) • T87
ACTIVITY ❷ **Making a Speed Graph**	🕘 35 MIN	👥 PAIRS	• *Student Activity Book*, pp. 8–10 • T88–T89 • Tape
DISCUSSION ❸ **Comparing Speed Graphs**	🕒 15 MIN	👥 CLASS	• *Student Activity Book*, pp. 8–10
SESSION FOLLOW-UP ❹ **Daily Practice and Homework**			• *Student Activity Book*, pp. 11–12 • *Student Math Handbook*, pp. 75–76 • M13–M14, Family Letter*

*See *Materials to Prepare*, p. 25.

Ten-Minute Math

Quick Survey For the survey, ask the class "What did you eat for breakfast this morning?" or whatever categorical question provides data that can be compared with the previous session's data. Add today's data to the bar graph created in the previous session and ask students to make comparisons. Ask students:

• What do you notice about the data?

• How are the data the same as yesterday's data?

• How are they different?

• What does that tell us about our class?

DISCUSSION
① The Motion Graph

10 MIN   **CLASS**

Math Focus Points for Discussion

◆ Interpreting the points and shape of a graph in terms of the situation the graph represents

Students should bring *Student Activity Book* pages 5–6 to this discussion. Invite volunteers to share the running stories they wrote for The Motion Graph. Display the transparency of The Motion Graph (T87) so that students can point to particular parts of the graph as they tell their story. After each volunteer's story, ask the class:

Does anybody have a question about how the graph and the story are related?

Work with students to clarify their understanding of the relationship between the graph of the runner's speed and the story. Repeat the process with another volunteer. Then ask whether students have stories that are different from the ones they heard, and resolve any differences in students' interpretations of the graph.

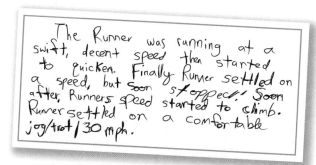

Sample Student Work

How did you know the runner "started to quicken"? Where did the runner stop? How can you tell that from the graph? What happened at the section marked a? How would you compare what's happening at a to what's happening at c and at g?

Students may point out that because there are no numbers on the graph, they can have different theories about actual speeds. For example, the speed at *a* could be relatively slow or relatively fast. What they can tell for sure is *relative* speed (e.g., that the speed at *c* is greater than the speed at *a* and that the speed at *a* is greater than the speed at *g*).

Penny Jars and Plant Growth

The Boston Marathon (page 1 of 2)

Participating in the Boston Marathon—all 26.2 miles of it—is an incredible experience. You're with thousands of other people, going through all kinds of different towns and cities and college campuses. Wheelchair participants get a lot of attention in Boston. People know us and they start us right at the front.

In the beginning of the race, there's about 4 miles of downhill. Like most wheelchair participants, I wheeled very fast on that downhill part. It felt good. But at mile 4, I remembered to pace myself. I slowed down a bit. For the next 9 miles or so, I wheeled nice and steady.

But then a very exciting thing happened. At Wellesley College, there was a huge crowd of students lining the course, screaming and clapping like crazy. All that excitement made me push faster and faster through the mile-long part of Wellesley. But then I noticed I was tired—too tired for being just a little more than halfway through the race. I stopped for a few seconds to get some water and pour some over my head. (I was getting hot, too!) I knew the hardest part of the race was coming up.

After Wellesley, I wheeled steadily for a few more miles. But then, by the seventeenth mile, it started getting hard. From mile 17 to 21 or so, I could feel myself gradually slowing down. There's a bunch of hard hills, and I knew I just had to take it easy to make it over those hills. My arms were aching so much. But the funny thing was, even once I had made it over the hills, I kept pushing slowly.

T88

▲ **Transparencies, T88**

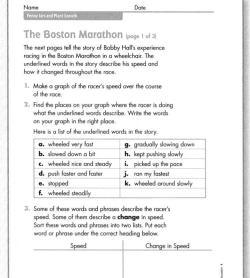

Penny Jars and Plant Growth

The Boston Marathon (page 2 of 2)

I think by 21 miles, I was running out of steam. It was hard to keep picking up my arms. Between 21 and 25 miles, I kept pushing slowly.

By 25 miles, I knew I would make it and I picked up the pace. The crowd was tremendous in the last mile or so. They just wouldn't let you slow down. The final stretch of a quarter mile or so is downhill, and I actually ran my fastest for that stretch. My arms felt all beaten up and shaky at the finish—but I wheeled around slowly for a while afterwards. That helps you keep from getting so stiff the next day.

—Bobby Hall (from a telephone interview)

T89

▲ **Transparencies, T89**

Name _____ Date _____

Penny Jars and Plant Growth

The Boston Marathon (page 1 of 3)

The next pages tell the story of Bobby Hall's experience racing in the Boston Marathon in a wheelchair. The underlined words in the story describe his speed and how it changed throughout the race.

1. Make a graph of the racer's speed over the course of the race.

2. Find the places on your graph where the racer is doing what the underlined words describe. Write the words on your graph in the right place.

Here is a list of the underlined words in the story.

a.	wheeled very fast	**g.**	gradually slowing down
b.	slowed down a bit	**h.**	kept pushing slowly
c.	wheeled nice and steady	**i.**	picked up the pace
d.	push faster and faster	**j.**	ran my fastest
e.	stopped	**k.**	wheeled around slowly
f.	wheeled steadily		

3. Some of these words and phrases describe the racer's speed. Some of them describe a **change** in speed. Sort these words and phrases into two lists. Put each word or phrase under the correct heading below.

Speed	Change in Speed

8   Unit 9   Session 1.2

▲ **Student Activity Book, p. 8**

ACTIVITY

② Making a Speed Graph

35 MIN   PAIRS

The class now works with a speed graph from a different point of view: instead of making a story to go with a graph, they make a graph to go with a story.

I'm going to read a story written by someone who has been a wheelchair racer in the Boston Marathon. Later in the session you will have a copy of this story to work with. For now, listen carefully for particular words that tell how the racer's speed changes during the race.

Display and read the transparencies of The Boston Marathon (T88–T89), so that students can follow along with you. Ask students what words they hear that describe the speed of the racer (e.g., *wheeled very fast, slowed down a bit, faster and faster*).

When several terms have been mentioned, ask students which of these terms describe speed and which describe *changes* in speed.

Before students begin work on the *Student Activity Book* pages, help them get paper ready for drawing their graph of the race. Distribute two sheets of paper to each pair and have students tape the sheets together along the short side so that they have enough space for the graph. (Some pairs may extend the graph by adding a third sheet of paper.) Then have students work in pairs on *Student Activity Book* pages 8–10.

Students work together to make a graph of the racer's changing speeds.

In this activity, students examine phrases in the marathon story and sort them into two categories: those about speed and those about changes in speed. Then they make a graph of the racer's speed based on the story, writing the phrases on corresponding parts of the graph. Each student should complete the lists on *Student Activity Book* page 8, but pairs can work together to complete a graph.

ONGOING ASSESSMENT: Observing Students at Work

Students classify words and phrases as describing speed or changes in speed, and sketch a graph that depicts the action in the story.

- **Are students drawing graphs of speed and not the shape of the landscape of the race?**

- **Are students sketching parts of the graph that match the descriptions of speed, such as *ran my fastest,* and changes in speed, such as *gradually slowing down*?**

As you circulate, pose questions that connect the shape of a graph with the terms.

- What would "stopped" (or "slowing quickly," or "slowing gradually," or "wheeled steadily") look like on a graph of speed?

Remind students to place the words about speed and changes in speed along the appropriate portions of the graph.

- What part of the graph shows "ran my fastest"? (or "picked up the pace," or other phrases)

As you watch students work, choose one or two graphs for the whole-group discussion.

DIFFERENTIATION: Supporting the Range of Learners

Intervention If some students are thinking of the graph as a picture of the geography of the course, remind them that just as the temperature graph showed how temperature increased, decreased, or stayed the same, this graph shows how speed increases, decreases, or stays the same. It is helpful to relate this kind of graph to students' own experiences. For example, ask a student to tell a story about walking and running. Sketch a graph about the student's story, emphasizing how his or her speed is changing.

▲ Student Activity Book, p. 9

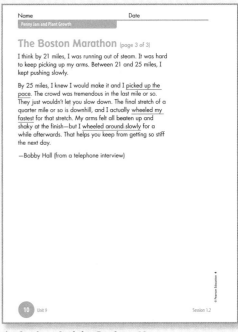

▲ Student Activity Book, p. 10

Students who are having difficulty with the quantity of information in the story can draw a graph for a portion of the story, such as the second paragraph. Some students may benefit from assigning possible number values to the speeds.

Students who need large amounts of room for writing can label their graphs using the letters given in the list on the *Student Activity Book* in place of the underlined phrases.

ELL Preview the story with English Language Learners. Show pictures or video clips of the Boston Marathon (or a similar race), as well as pictures of wheelchair racing. Discuss how someone in a wheelchair can participate in a race. As you read the story, make quick sketches and/or use gestures to help students comprehend it. Pause frequently and ask students to summarize what they have heard. Before students begin work on *Student Activity Book* page 8, check for understanding by asking them to interpret the listed phrases with gestures or in their own words.

DISCUSSION

15 MIN CLASS

③ Comparing Speed Graphs

Math Focus Points for Discussion

◆ Interpreting the points and shape of a graph in terms of the situation the graph represents

◆ Discriminating between features of a graph that represent quantity and those that represent changes in quantity

Post all of the graphs in the room for students to examine.

Invite a few students to point out parts of their graph that match the language of the story, and have them explain their thinking.

Questions such as these can focus the discussion:

• How do you show the racer wheeling slowly? How does this compare to the way you showed him moving faster? What does "stop" look like on your graph?

• How did you show him pushing faster and faster? How did you show him slowing down? What does "picking up the pace" look like? How does "changing pace" look different from "going at a steady pace"?

- "Wheeled nice and steady" and "wheeled steadily" seem to mean the same thing. How does your graph show this?

- Does anyone's graph show a difference between stopping suddenly to get a drink and slowing down gradually because the racer is tired?

Students identify portions of the graph that correspond to specific passages in the story.

SESSION FOLLOW-UP

Daily Practice and Homework

 Daily Practice: For ongoing review, have students complete *Student Activity Book* page 11.

 Homework: Students interpret information in a table about temperature and sketch a graph on *Student Activity Book* page 12.

 Student Math Handbook: Students and families may use *Student Math Handbook* pages 75–76 for reference and review. See pages 163–166 in the back of this unit.

 Family Letter: Send home copies of the Family Letter (M13–M14).

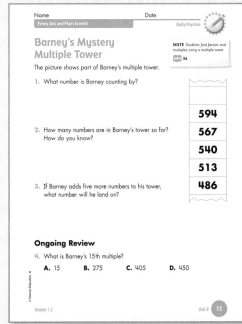

Name _____ Date _____

Penny Jars and Plant Growth — Daily Practice

Barney's Mystery Multiple Tower

NOTE Students find factors and multiples using a multiple tower.

Unit 36

The picture shows part of Barney's multiple tower.

1. What number is Barney counting by?

2. How many numbers are in Barney's tower so far? How do you know?

| 594 |
| 567 |
| 540 |
| 513 |
| 486 |

3. If Barney adds five more numbers to his tower, what number will he land on?

Ongoing Review

4. What is Barney's 15th multiple?

   A. 15   **B.** 275   **C.** 405   **D.** 450

Session 1.2 — Unit 9 — 11

▲ **Student Activity Book, p. 11**

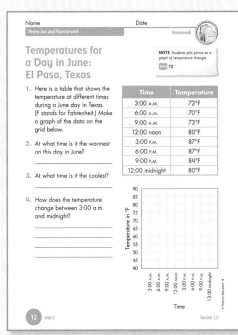

Name _____ Date _____

Penny Jars and Plant Growth — Homework

Temperatures for a Day in June: El Paso, Texas

NOTE Students plot points on a graph of temperature changes.

Unit 72

1. Here is a table that shows the temperature at different times during a June day in Texas. (F stands for Fahrenheit.) Make a graph of the data on the grid below.

2. At what time is it the warmest on this day in June?

3. At what time is it the coolest?

Time	Temperature
3:00 A.M.	72°F
6:00 A.M.	70°F
9:00 A.M.	73°F
12:00 noon	80°F
3:00 P.M.	87°F
6:00 P.M.	87°F
9:00 P.M.	84°F
12:00 midnight	80°F

4. How does the temperature change between 3:00 a.m. and midnight?

12 — Unit 9 — Session 1.2

▲ **Student Activity Book, p. 12**

Mathematical Emphases

Using Tables and Graphs Using graphs to represent change

Math Focus Points

◆ Identifying points in a graph with corresponding values in a table and interpreting the numerical information in terms of the situation the graph represents

◆ Plotting points on a coordinate grid to represent a situation in which one quantity is changing in relation to another

◆ Comparing situations by describing the differences in their graphs

◆ Describing the relative steepness of graphs or parts of graphs in terms of different rates of change

Using Tables and Graphs Using tables to represent change

Math Focus Points

◆ Using tables to represent the relationship between two quantities in a situation of constant change

◆ Interpreting numbers in a table in terms of the situation they represent

Linear Change Describing and representing a constant rate of change

Math Focus Points

◆ Finding the value of one quantity in a situation of constant change, given the value of the other

◆ Creating a representation for a situation of constant change

◆ Describing the relationship between two quantities in a situation of constant change, taking into account a beginning amount and a constant increase

◆ Writing an arithmetic expression for finding the value of one quantity in terms of the other in a situation of constant change

◆ Making rules that relate one variable to another in situations of constant change

◆ Using symbolic letter notation to represent the value of one variable in terms of another

Penny Jars and Towers

SESSION 2.1 p. 46	Student Activity Book	Student Math Handbook	Professional Development: Read Ahead of Time	
The Penny Jar Students determine how values change in the Penny Jar, a situation of constant change. They create representations that show the starting amount, the amount added each round, and the total amount.	13–15	78–79	• **Teacher Note:** Situations with a Constant Rate of Change: Linear Functions, p. 138 • **Teacher Note:** Representing a Constant Rate of Change, p. 140 • **Part 4: Ten-Minute Math** in *Implementing Investigations in Grade 4:* Closest Estimate	
SESSION 2.2 **p. 54**				
Penny Jar Tables Students continue to work with situations of constant change as they develop methods for finding the number of pennies in the Penny Jar after skipping several rounds. They use tables to record their work.	17–20	78–80	• **Dialogue Box:** "I took a guess that there was a pattern," p. 154	
SESSION 2.3 **p. 61**				
Round 20 Students record calculations for a new Penny Jar situation. They develop arguments and representations to show how Round 20 is related to Round 10.	21–24	79–80	• **Dialogue Box:** Doubling or Not?, p. 156	
SESSION 2.4 **p. 68**				
Penny Jar Graphs Students construct graphs and tables that show situations of constant change. They share their expressions for Round 100 of a Penny Jar situation and write a rule for any round, using words and symbolic notation.	25–31	81, 86		
SESSION 2.5 **p. 76**				
Assessment: Penny Jar Comparisons Students use tables, graphs, and arithmetic expressions to represent and compare situations of constant change. They use the Penny Jar context as well as a new context—Windows and Towers. During Math Workshop, students are assessed on their understanding of tables and graphs.	33–39	82–85		

Materials to Gather	Materials to Prepare
• **Clear jar** • **Pennies or counters** (46; 50 per pair, optional) • **Blank transparencies** (5 or 6, optional) • **Overhead markers** (optional)	• **M19, Penny Jar Situation Cards** Make copies, then cut apart. (1 per pair)
• **M19, Penny Jar Situation Cards** (from Session 2.1) • **T94–T95, Penny Jar Table** 🖨 • **Pennies or counters** (50 per pair)	• **M20–M21, Penny Jar Table** Make copies. (1 per student)
• **T96, Penny Jar Table with Calculation** 🖨	
• **M19, Penny Jar Situation Cards** (from Session 2.1) • **T97, Penny Jar Graphs 1 and 2** 🖨 • **T98, Blank Penny Jar Graph** 🖨 • **Grid paper** (optional) • **Scissors** (1 per pair) • **Glue or tape**	• **M23, Penny Jar Tables A and B** Make copies. (1 per student)
• **Connecting cubes** (50 per pair)	• **Chart paper** Create a two-column chart with the headings "Number of Floors" in the left column and "Number of Windows" in the right column. Create ten rows under these headings. Write the numbers from 1 to 10 under Number of Floors, with 1 at the top of the table and 10 at the bottom. • **M26, Penny Jar Comparison Cards** Make copies, then cut apart. (1 per pair) • **M27, Assessment Checklist: Penny Jar Comparisons** ☑ Make copies. (as needed)

🖨 Overhead Transparency   ☑ Checklist Available

Penny Jars and Towers,
continued

	Student Activity Book	Student Math Handbook	Professional Development: Read Ahead of Time	
SESSION 2.6 p. 84				
Can There Be 15 Windows? Students work with different situations of constant change using tables, graphs, and arithmetic expressions. They determine whether a particular value can occur in a particular situation of constant change.	33–37, 41–48	80–81		
SESSION 2.7 p. 91				
Comparing Penny Jar Situations Students continue working with tables, graphs, arithmetic expressions, and symbolic notation to describe and compare situations of constant change. They discuss how parallel, intersecting, or diverging graphs show the relationship between two Penny Jar situations.	35–37, 41–46, 49–51	82–85	• **Dialogue Box:** Comparing Penny Jars, p. 158	
SESSION 2.8 p. 97				
Rules for Windows and Towers Students determine a rule for each of four kinds of towers, using words and symbolic notation.	33–34, 43–44, 53–57	86	• **Dialogue Box:** Rules for the Double Tower, p. 160	

Materials to Gather	Materials to Prepare
• **M26, Penny Jar Comparison Cards** (from Session 2.5) • **M27, Assessment Checklist: Penny Jar Comparisons** ✓ (optional) • **Connecting cubes** (50 per pair)	• **M28–M30, Penny Jar Comparisons** Make copies. (as needed; up to 3 per pair)
• **M26, Penny Jar Comparison Cards** (from Session 2.5) • **M28–M30, Penny Jar Comparisons** (remaining copies from Session 2.6) • **T99–T102, Penny Jar Comparison Cards: Graphs** 🖵 • **Connecting cubes** (50 per pair) • **Chart paper** (4 sheets, optional)	
• **Connecting cubes** (50 per pair or group) • **Grid paper** (as needed)	• **Chart paper** Write a different title on four separate sheets: "Single Tower," "Double Tower," "Square Tower," and "Corner Tower." Post these sheets where students can write on them easily.

🖵 Overhead Transparency   ✓ Checklist Available

The Penny Jar

Math Focus Points

◈ Finding the value of one quantity in a situation of constant change, given the value of the other (e.g., if you know the number of the round, what is the total number of pennies?)

◈ Creating a representation for a situation of constant change

Vocabulary

table
representation

Today's Plan

	Materials
ACTIVITY **① Introducing Penny Jar Situations** 20 MIN · CLASS · PAIRS	• *Student Activity Book*, p. 13 • M19* • A clear jar; pennies or counters
ACTIVITY **② How Many After Each Round?** 20 MIN · PAIRS	• *Student Activity Book*, p. 13 • Blank transparencies; overhead markers; pennies or counters
DISCUSSION **③ Sharing Representations** 20 MIN · CLASS	
SESSION FOLLOW-UP **④ Daily Practice and Homework**	• *Student Activity Book*, pp. 14–15 • *Student Math Handbook*, pp. 78–79

*See *Materials to Prepare*, p. 43.

Ten-Minute Math

Closest Estimate Show Problems 1, 2, and 3 on *Closest Estimate* (T90) one at a time. Give students approximately 30 seconds to look at the three possible estimates that are provided and determine which is closest to the actual answer. Have two or three students explain their reasoning for each problem.

How did you break the numbers apart?

How did you determine the magnitude of your answer?

If you changed the numbers in the problem, how did you change them, and why?

Is the closest estimate greater than or less than the actual answer?

How do you know?

20 MIN · CLASS · PAIRS

ACTIVITY

Introducing Penny Jar Situations

Let students know that they will be continuing their work with graphs and tables over the next 8 sessions, but that they will be working with situations that are different from those in Investigation 1 (speed and temperature). As they work, students might start thinking about these new situations and how they are different.

Today we are going to talk about Penny Jars. In a Penny Jar exercise, you have a jar containing some pennies. Then you put a certain number of pennies into the jar, again and again. ❶ ❷

Students who used *Investigations* in Grade 1 may be familiar with the Penny Jar context.

Let's start with this jar. It has 4 pennies in it. [Show the jar to students.] We'll put 6 pennies in the jar during each round. [Put 6 pennies in the jar.] How many pennies are in the jar now?

Continue through 7 rounds (46 pennies in all). After each round, have the class identify the number of pennies in the jar. Keep track of the values by writing them in a list on the board. ❸

> Begin with 4 pennies.
>
> Add 6 pennies each round.

You might also draw a quick sketch of the pennies in the jar after each round to help students visualize what is happening. ❹

Distribute two of the prepared cards from Penny Jar Situation Cards (M19) to each pair. Student pairs find the number of pennies after 6 rounds for each of the two situations and record their work on *Student Activity Book* page 13.

Professional Development

❶ **Teacher Note:** Situations with a Constant Rate of Change: Linear Functions, p. 138

❷ **Teacher Note:** Representing a Constant Rate of Change, p. 140

Teaching Notes

❸ **Representing Data** Note that tables are not introduced explicitly until Session 2.2, after students have a chance to create their own representations for Penny Jar situations in this session.

❹ **Visualizing Data** In the picture, the pennies added each round are sketched in an array. This emphasizes the constant change in the situation and its relationship to multiplication. Visualizing what is happening in the jar in this way can help students develop generalizations about how the total number of pennies in the jar is related to the number of rounds. This will be discussed beginning in the next session.

Penny Jars and Plant Growth

Closest Estimate (page 1 of 4)

1. $89 \times 32 \approx$	300	3,000	3,200
2. $6 \times 109 \approx$	160	600	700
3. $200 \div 18 \approx$	10	15	20
4. $450 \div 49 \approx$	5	10	100
5. $15\overline{)294} \approx$	20	200	4,500
6. $6\overline{)371} \approx$	6	60	600

T90

▲ Transparencies, T90

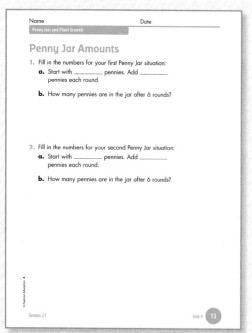

▲ Resource Masters, M19

▲ Student Activity Book, p. 13

ONGOING ASSESSMENT: Observing Students at Work

Students determine the number of pennies after 6 rounds for each Penny Jar situation, given the starting number and the number of pennies added in each round.

- **Do students correctly interpret their Penny Jar situation (i.e., do they use the start number once and then repeatedly add the other number)?**

- **Do students find the amount for each successive round, or do they realize that they can use multiplication to determine the 6th round amount without listing every round?**

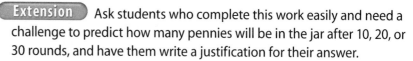

DIFFERENTIATION: Supporting the Range of Learners

Extension   Ask students who complete this work easily and need a challenge to predict how many pennies will be in the jar after 10, 20, or 30 rounds, and have them write a justification for their answer.

ELL   If students are not sure about the meaning of the word *round,* help them apply it to this context by using a situation with which they are familiar. This may include comparing each round to a turn (as in a game) to an inning in a baseball game, or to an action taken each day or each week.

ACTIVITY

2 How Many After Each Round?

20 MIN   PAIRS

Once you have the sense that students understand the Penny Jar, interrupt their pair work briefly to focus their continuing work on a new question. You do not need to wait until every group has completed *Student Activity Book* page 13 before posing this question. Students can continue to work on that page with this new question in mind.

Look at your work on the *Student Activity Book* page. You have been finding how many pennies there are after 6 rounds. Can you tell from your work how many pennies there are in the jar after each round? That is the next question you will work on. Once you have finished the questions on the student sheet, choose one of the Penny Jar situations on your sheet and find a way to show on a separate sheet of paper the number of pennies in the jar after each round. You can use a picture, a table, a diagram, numbers, or any other way that shows this clearly. Someone should be able to look at what you draw and easily see how many pennies there are after any round. If you have time, you can show more than 6 rounds.

Students work together to find a method of representing the number of pennies in the jar after each round.

ONGOING ASSESSMENT: Observing Students at Work

Students make representations of Penny Jar situations using diagrams, pictures, tables, or graphs that show the number of pennies after each round.

- **Do students create a representation that communicates the number of pennies in the jar after each round?**

- **Can students describe how their representation shows the starting number, the amount added each round, and the total after a certain number of rounds?**

While students are working, ask them to explain their representations:

If I wanted to know how many pennies are in the jar after round 3, how would I find that on your representation?

Also ask how the starting number and the amount added each time are included in their representation. As you circulate, select three or four different kinds of representations for the class to look at together during the next discussion. The pairs that created them can redraw their representations on overhead transparencies, or you or the students can sketch large versions of them on the board.

DIFFERENTIATION: Supporting the Range of Learners

Intervention If students are having difficulty thinking of a representation, suggest that they use counters or pennies and arrange them to show the start, the first round, the second round, etc. Then ask them whether they can capture their arrangement of pennies in a drawing or in some other way on paper. Pennies or counters should remain available throughout this investigation for those students who benefit from acting out these situations with concrete materials. Most students will not need to use them.

DISCUSSION

③ Sharing Representations

20 MIN   CLASS

Math Focus Points for Discussion

◆ Creating a representation for a situation of constant change

Be sure to include a variety of students' representations for this discussion: diagrams and lists of numbers, as well as tables and graphs, if available. If one group has offered a list of numbers as a representation, display the table representation immediately following that one so that students can compare them.

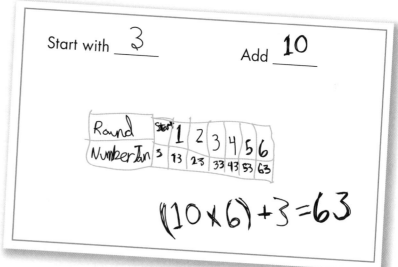

Sample Student Work

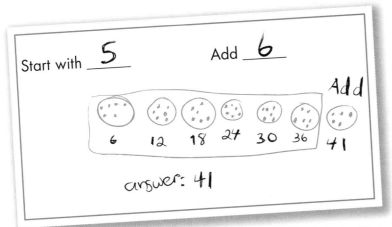

Start with ___5___   Add ___6___

6   12   18   24   30   36   41

Add

answer: 41

Sample Student Work

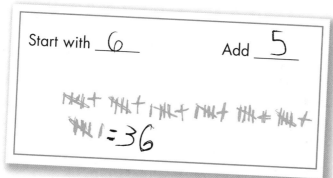

Start with ___6___   Add ___5___

=36

Sample Student Work

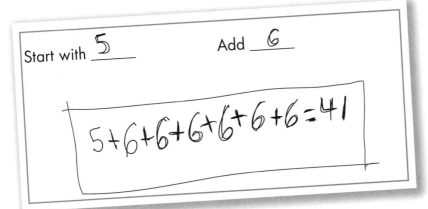

Start with ___5___   Add ___6___

$5+6+6+6+6+6+6=41$

Sample Student Work

For each representation, ask:

- When you look at this representation, can you tell how many pennies are in the Penny Jar after round 2? After round 3? After round 4? How many pennies were in the Penny Jar at the start? How many pennies were added each round?

- What helps you see how many pennies were in the jar after each round? What helps you see how many were added each round?

Introduce the idea of using arithmetic expressions to describe the number of pennies:

Suppose we start with 4 and add 9 each round. What arithmetic expressions can you use to represent the number of pennies in the jar after round 6?

Students might say:

 "I would write it as 4 + 9 + 9 + 9 + 9 + 9 + 9."

 " I would say 4 + (6 × 9). "

If students do not seem to understand your question, start at the beginning of the situation and ask for an arithmetic expression for each round:

Let's think about this situation: start with 7. Add 3 each round. How many pennies are in the jar at the beginning? How would you figure out how many pennies are in the jar after the first round? The second round?

Help students understand the process as a series of addition problems:

Start   7

Round 1   7 + 3

Round 2   7 + 3 + 3

Round 3   7 + 3 + 3 + 3

At the end of the session, post all of the representations so that students can refer to them during this Investigation.

SESSION FOLLOW-UP

Daily Practice and Homework

 Daily Practice: For ongoing review, have students complete *Student Activity Book* page 14.

 Homework: Students write a story and make a graph about changing speed on *Student Activity Book* page 15.

 Student Math Handbook: Students and families may use *Student Math Handbook* pages 78–79 for reference and review. See pages 163–166 in the back of this unit.

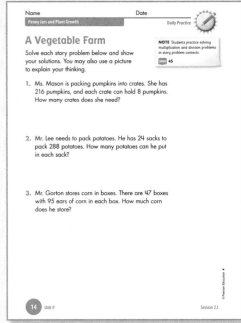

▲ **Student Activity Book, p. 14**

▲ **Student Activity Book, p. 15**

Penny Jar Tables

Math Focus Points

- Finding the value of one quantity in a situation of constant change, given the value of the other (e.g., if you know the number of the round, what is the total number of pennies?)

- Using tables to represent the relationship between two quantities in a situation of constant change

- Interpreting numbers in a table in terms of the situation they represent

- Describing the relationship between two quantities in a situation of constant change, taking into account a beginning amount and a constant increase

Today's Plan		Materials
ACTIVITY ❶ **Penny Jar Tables**	30 MIN · CLASS · PAIRS	• *Student Activity Book,* pp. 17–18 • M19 (from Session 2.1); M20–M21*; T94–T95 • Pennies or counters
DISCUSSION ❷ **Start with 2 and Add 3**	30 MIN · CLASS · PAIRS	• M20–M21*
SESSION FOLLOW-UP ❸ **Daily Practice and Homework**		• *Student Activity Book,* pp. 19–20 • *Student Math Handbook,* pp. 78–80

*See *Materials to Prepare,* p. 43.

Ten-Minute Math

Closest Estimate Show Problems 4, 5, and 6 on *Closest Estimate* (T90) one at a time. Give students approximately 30 seconds to look at the three possible estimates that are provided and determine which is closest to the actual answer. Have two or three students explain their reasoning for each problem.

How did you break the numbers apart?

How did you determine the magnitude of your answer?

If you changed the numbers in the problem, how did you change them, and why?

Is the closest estimate greater than or less than the actual answer?

How do you know?

ACTIVITY

Penny Jar Tables

30 MIN   CLASS   PAIRS

In this activity, students continue to work with Penny Jar Situation Cards (M19) to determine the total number of pennies in the jar after a particular round. Students work on answering questions such as "How many pennies will be in the jar after round 10?" They begin to develop methods for figuring out the total number of pennies without totaling every round up to that point.

Introduce this activity with an example. Display the transparency of Penny Jar Table (T94), and work with the class on the situation "Start with 2 pennies. Add 3 pennies each round." Complete the table through round 3 or 4. (Do not fill in the entire table at this time.)

Number of Rounds	Total Number of Pennies
Start with	2
1	5
2	8
3	11
4	14
5	
6	
7	
10	
15	
20	

Notice that a few rows down, the table skips from round 7 to round 10, and then from round 10 to round 15 and from round 15 to round 20. When you work on this sheet, think about whether you can figure out the number of pennies for round 10 without having to list all of the rounds between rounds 7 and 10.

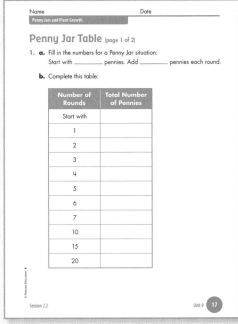

▲ Student Activity Book, p. 17; Resource Masters, M20; T94

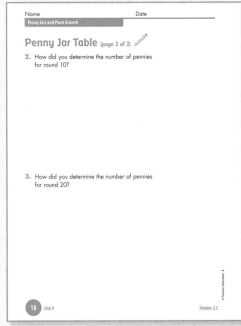

▲ Student Activity Book, p. 18; Resource Masters, M21; T95

Students now choose a Penny Jar situation from the Penny Jar Situation Cards (M19) and begin *Student Activity Book* pages 17–18. As students work, ask them how they are determining the number of pennies in the first seven rounds.

Can you say how to determine the total number of pennies in round 7 without referring to round 6? How many (3s) do you need to add for the seventh round? Is there a way to think of that using multiplication?

Students determine the number of pennies in each round shown on the table.

ONGOING ASSESSMENT: Observing Students at Work

Students determine the number of pennies for a given round later in the sequence.

- **Do students interpret the situation and use the table correctly for the first 7 rounds?**

- **How do students determine the total for round 10?** Do they figure out the amounts for rounds 8 and 9? Do they reason that the total number of pennies in round 10 must increase by 3 times the amount added in each round?

- **Are students using multiplication and/or addition in order to determine the totals for rounds 15 and 20?**

As you circulate, ask groups to explain how they can determine the number of pennies in the jar after round 10, reminding students that the table jumps from round 7 to round 10. When the table skips rounds, many students at first determine the number of pennies for each round missing from the table—in this case, rounds 8 and 9. Have pennies or counters available for students to use as necessary. As students continue working, encourage them to think of ways they can determine the number of pennies in the rounds indicated on the table without figuring out each intervening round. Some students will still list all rounds in order to determine round 20, but other students will begin to think through other methods—some that work and some that do not.

Students often try to follow characteristics of the number sequence they see in the table. These patterns are compelling, but they can take students' attention away from how the table reflects what is happening in the Penny Jar situation.❶

Professional Development

❶ **Dialogue Box:** "I took a guess that there was a pattern," p. 154

DIFFERENTIATION: Supporting the Range of Learners

Intervention In order to see how the total number of pennies increases over several rounds, some students may find it useful to make a representation like the one they created in Session 2.1. Others may find it useful to write out the arithmetic expression that shows a calculation for each round next to the appropriate row in the table. For example:

Number of Rounds	Total Number of Pennies	
Start with	3	
1	8	3+5
2	13	3+5+5
3	18	3+5+5+5

Sample Student Work

Students may use addition, as shown in the table above, or multiplication: $3 + (1 \times 5)$, $3 + (2 \times 5)$, $3 + (3 \times 5)$, and so forth.

If students use addition to determine the amounts for rounds 10, 15, and 20, ask them whether they can think of a way to write a shorter expression using multiplication.

If some students are not clear about how to read and interpret a table, work with them to establish meaning for what each column represents and what the values in each row represent.

Extension Students who finish early and can find the totals for all rounds easily can create another Penny Jar situation on a copy of Penny Jar Table (M20–M21), using numbers that are challenging for them. Here are some examples you can suggest:

1. *Start with 3 pennies and add 75 pennies each time.*

2. *Start with 2 pennies and add 99 pennies each time.*

Students can also find the number of pennies after 30 rounds, 40 rounds, or 50 rounds.

DISCUSSION

Start with 2 and Add 3

30 MIN   CLASS   PAIRS

Math Focus Points for Discussion

◆ Describing the relationship between two quantities in a situation of constant change, taking into account a beginning amount and a constant increase

◆ Finding the value of one quantity in a situation of constant change, given the value of the other (e.g., if you know the number of the round, what is the total number of pennies?)

Gather the class together, and return to the Penny Jar situation from the beginning of class: Start with 2 pennies. Add 3 pennies each round. Have students work in pairs to complete a new copy of Penny Jar Table (M20–M21) for this Penny Jar situation.

Using the transparency of the Penny Jar table that you partially filled in at the beginning of the session, solicit student responses to complete rounds 1 through 7.

What is the number for round 10? How did you determine it?

Continue completing the table for rounds 15 and 20, asking for a variety of explanations for each.

Students might say:

"I figured out that round 11 is 35, and then added 3, so round 12 is 38, round 13 is 41, round 14 is 44, and round 15 is 47."

"It was 5 more rounds to get to round 15, so you'd have 3 more pennies each time—that's 3 × 5, or 15 pennies, so we added 15 pennies to what we had for round 10."

If students seem ready to articulate a general rule for any number of rounds, ask them to express their ideas in words.❷ Then encourage class discussion of the proposed rule:

So Jill has an idea about how to find the number of pennies for any round for this Penny Jar. I'm going to record her idea on the board. [Write idea on board.] What do you think about this idea? Do you think that Jill's rule will work for any round? Why do you think so?

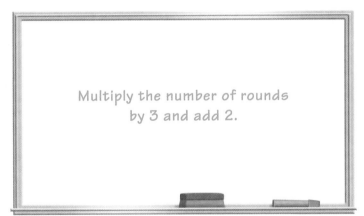

Multiply the number of rounds by 3 and add 2.

You will come back to articulating general rules and notation for these rules in Sessions 2.3 and 2.4.

If you have time, spend just a few minutes on a new type of problem that this Investigation refers to as a "backward problem" because it begins with the total number and poses a question about the number of rounds:

Will this Penny Jar—starting with 2 pennies and adding 3 pennies each round—ever have exactly 90 pennies in it at the end of a round? See if you can think of a way to answer this question without figuring out every round. Is there something about the number 90 that would help you decide whether there can ever be that number of pennies in the jar?❸

Math Notes

❷ **Doubling** A common incorrect strategy that students may propose is doubling the number of pennies in one round (for example, round 10) to get the number of pennies in twice as many rounds (for example, round 20). This method works for only one of the Penny Jar situations: Start with 0 pennies/Add 8 each round. If doubling comes up in this discussion, help students notice that doubling the amount does not lead to the same result as the other methods that students are using. If some students notice that doubling does work for the situation in which they start with 0 pennies, ask students to keep thinking about why it works in that case. Let them know that you will discuss this idea further in the next session.

❸ **Multiples of 3 and Counting by 3** Students sometimes look at a Penny Jar situation such as "Start with 2 pennies/Add 3 pennies each round" and refer to the sequence of numbers as "multiples of 3." They notice the pattern of increasing by 3 and use vocabulary that they commonly associate with counting by 3s. Ask students how this Penny Jar situation is similar to the multiples of 3 and how it is different. Since this Penny Jar situation does not start at zero, the results are not multiples of 3. However, the number sequence produced by this Penny Jar situation and the sequence of multiples of 3 both have a constant increase of 3.

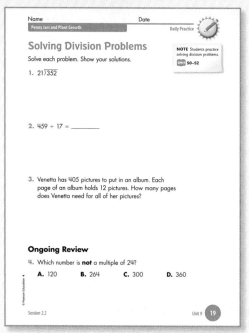

Name _____ **Date** _____

Penny Jars and Plant Growth

Daily Practice

Solving Division Problems

Solve each problem. Show your solutions.

NOTE Students practice solving division problems.
SMH 50–52

1. 21⟌352

2. 459 ÷ 17 = _____

3. Venetta has 405 pictures to put in an album. Each page of an album holds 12 pictures. How many pages does Venetta need for all of her pictures?

Ongoing Review

4. Which number is **not** a multiple of 24?

   A. 120   **B.** 264   **C.** 300   **D.** 360

Session 2.2   Unit 9 **19**

▲ **Student Activity Book, p. 19**

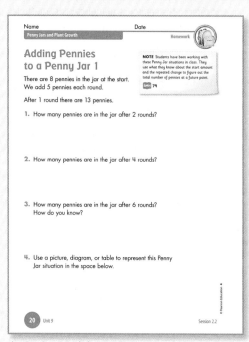

Name _____ **Date** _____

Penny Jars and Plant Growth

Homework

Adding Pennies to a Penny Jar 1

There are 8 pennies in the jar at the start. We add 5 pennies each round.

After 1 round there are 13 pennies.

NOTE Students have been working with these Penny Jar situations in class. They use what they know about the start amount and the repeated change to figure out the total number of pennies at a future point.
SMH 79

1. How many pennies are in the jar after 2 rounds?

2. How many pennies are in the jar after 4 rounds?

3. How many pennies are in the jar after 6 rounds? How do you know?

4. Use a picture, diagram, or table to represent this Penny Jar situation in the space below.

20 Unit 9   Session 2.2

▲ **Student Activity Book, p. 20**

Have students talk in pairs for a minute or two. Then solicit ideas from the class. This kind of question is another way to encourage thinking about how the two parts of this situation—the starting amount and the constant increase—affect the total amount. In this case, there can never be a multiple of 3 in the Penny Jar at the conclusion of a round because the total amount is always made up of some number of groups of 3 pennies plus the starting amount of 2 pennies. Do not expect all students to grasp this idea entirely during this discussion. These ideas will continue to build throughout the rest of the Investigation.

SESSION FOLLOW-UP

③ Daily Practice and Homework

Daily Practice: For ongoing review, have students complete _Student Activity Book_ page 19.

Homework: Students work on a Penny Jar situation on _Student Activity Book_ page 20.

Student Math Handbook: Students and families may use _Student Math Handbook_ pages 78–80 for reference and review. See pages 163–166 in the back of this unit.

Round 20

Math Focus Points

◆ Finding the value of one quantity in a situation of constant change, given the value of the other (e.g., if you know the number of the round, what is the total number of pennies?)

◆ Describing the relationship between two quantities in a situation of constant change, taking into account a beginning amount and a constant increase

◆ Writing an arithmetic expression for finding the value of one quantity in terms of the other in a situation of constant change

Today's Plan			Materials
1 ACTIVITY **Round 20**	35 MIN	PAIRS	• *Student Activity Book*, pp. 21–22 • T96
2 DISCUSSION **Comparing Rounds 10 and 20**	25 MIN	CLASS	• *Student Activity Book*, pp. 21–22
3 SESSION FOLLOW-UP **Daily Practice and Homework**			• *Student Activity Book*, pp. 23–24 • *Student Math Handbook*, pp. 79–80

Ten-Minute Math

Quick Survey For the survey, ask the class, "How many letters are in your first, middle, and last names?" or a different numerical question that you or the students choose. Make sure they collect data about something they already know or can observe easily. With today's data, make a line plot. Ask:

• What do you notice about the data?

• What do the data tell us about our class?

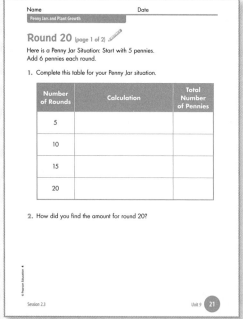

▲ Transparencies, T96

▲ Student Activity Book, p. 21

35 MIN   PAIRS

ACTIVITY

① Round 20

In this activity, students work with a Penny Jar situation, using a table to record every fifth round. Students explain how they found the number of pennies after round 20. They also develop arguments and a representation to show why the number of pennies for round 20 is *not* double the number of pennies for round 10.

Show students the Penny Jar Table with Calculation (T96). Work together as a class to model how to record information in the first two rows of the table for this Penny Jar situation: Start with 3 pennies. Add 5 pennies each round.

As you fill out this table, be sure to show how you found the total number of pennies in each round. Write your method in the middle column, *Calculation*. You don't have to use the same method for every round.

Unlike the tables students have used previously, this table does not include a row for the "start number." However, students still need to take this amount into account in their calculations. Collect several student suggestions for each calculation column, but do not spend time discussing them now.

Number of Rounds	Calculation	Total Number of Pennies
5	3 + 5 + 5 + 5 + 5 + 5	28
10	3 + 5 + 5 + 5 + 5 + 5 + 5 + 5 + 5 + 5 + 5 (10 × 5) + 3 28 + 28 − 3	53
15		
20		

You may come up with other ways to calculate that make sense to you as you work on today's activity.

Have students turn to *Student Activity Book* pages 21–22. Point out that they will be recording the total number of pennies for rounds 5, 10, 15, and 20 for the given Penny Jar situation.

As you listen and observe, choose two or three different methods for finding the number of pennies in round 20 for the whole-group discussion. These might include an addition strategy, a multiplication strategy, a doubling strategy that does not work (e.g., double the number of pennies in round 10), and a doubling strategy that does work (e.g., double the number of pennies in round 10 and subtract the start number).

ONGOING ASSESSMENT: Observing Students at Work

Students determine the total number of pennies for a given Penny Jar situation for every fifth round, record the calculations they are using, and consider whether the number of pennies in round 20 is double the number of pennies in round 10.

- **Can students write an arithmetic expression that shows how to calculate the total number of pennies?**

- **Are students using multiplication to show that the constant increase occurs for each round?** For example, do they use expressions such as $5 + (10 \times 6)$ for round 10?

- **Can students use their representations and tables to explain their thoughts about doubling the number of pennies for round 10 to determine the number for round 20?**

As students are working, ask them about their calculations for both round 10 and round 20.

- How did you take into account the number of pennies that were in the jar at the beginning?

- How did you take into account the number added each round?

- I notice you're using long addition strings for your arithmetic expression. Is there a way you can use multiplication to show the same thing with fewer numbers?

DIFFERENTIATION: Supporting the Range of Learners

Intervention Use the "Start with 0 pennies/Add 8 each round" card with students who are having difficulty taking into account both the starting amount and the amount of change. If students start with this card as a way into the activity, have them then do the activity a second time with a closely related situation, such as "Start with 2 pennies/Add 8 each round." Ask questions such as the following:

Since we started with 2 pennies in the jar instead of 0, what do you think will happen to the total number of pennies after 5 rounds?

Teaching Note

 Rules Some students may notice that there is a "rule" for finding the total number of pennies for any number of rounds. For example, "multiply the amount added each time by the number of rounds and add the starting amount." If some students are talking about this idea, encourage them to write this explanation on their paper and let them know that the class will be talking about rules like this again during the next session.

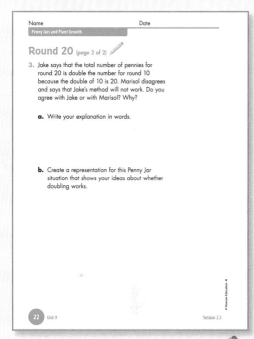

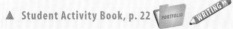
▲ Student Activity Book, p. 22

If students have difficulty finding the total number of pennies for every five rounds, help them build a visual representation. Consider using an arrangement of dots, showing the start number as a single row and the constant increase as an array. This can make the connection with multiplication clear, and can easily be constructed with coins or counters.

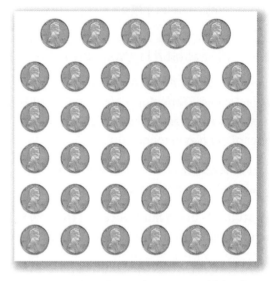

Start with 5 pennies. Add 6 each round.

Extension Students who need a challenge can think about how to modify the incorrect strategy of doubling the number of pennies in round 10 to get the number in round 20. Encourage them to write a rule that works to find the total number of pennies for any round. You can also pose "backward problems," such as "Will your Penny Jar ever have 96 pennies in it?"

DISCUSSION
② Comparing Rounds 10 and 20

25 MIN   CLASS

Math Focus Points for Discussion

◆ Writing an arithmetic expression for finding the value of one quantity in terms of the other in a situation of constant change

◆ Describing the relationship between two quantities in a situation of constant change, taking into account a beginning amount and a constant increase

First, call on students you observed during the previous activity and ask them to share their methods for finding the number of pennies after round 20. For each, write the calculation on the board. After each method is shared, include other students by asking:

Who else used a method similar to this one?

Methods that might be shared include:

- Begin with the start number and add on 6 for each round:
  $5 + 6 + 6 + 6 + 6 + 6 + 6 + 6 + \ldots$

- Multiply the number added each time by the number of rounds and add on the start number: $(20 \times 6) + 5$

- Add on to a previous amount: The number of pennies in 15 rounds is 95, so I added on 5 more rounds. $95 + (5 \times 6)$

Sample Student Work

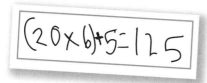

Sample Student Work

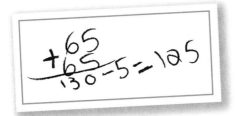

Sample Student Work

Teaching Note

❷ Doubling Strategies If you have time and your students have ideas, ask them how to modify a doubling strategy for this Penny Jar situation so that it does work. Here are some ideas students may offer:

1. Double the number of pennies in round 10, and then subtract the starting amount: $(65 \times 2) - 5$

2. Subtract the starting amount from the number of pennies in round 10, double it, and add the starting amount back in: $65 - 5 = 60$
$60 \times 2 = 120$ $120 + 5 = 125$

3. Subtract the starting amount from the number of pennies in round 10, and add that amount to the number of pennies in round 10:
$65 - 5 = 60$ $60 + 65 = 125$

Professional Development

❸ Dialogue Box: Doubling or Not?, p. 156

As each method is shared, ask how the starting amount and the amount added each time were taken into account. Establish that the number of pennies in the jar after round 20 is 125.

Focus the discussion on arguments about doubling the number of pennies for round 10 to find the number of pennies for round 20. At this point, it will probably be clear to most students that this method does not work, because doubling 65 does not result in 125. However, the question to be discussed is *why* this method does not work and what modifications to this approach are needed to make it work.❷

Doubling can be very useful in some situations. It seems at first that it should work here. Why doesn't it?

Ask students to explain their thinking by referring to their representations or numerical expressions. You may want to sketch some student representations on the board so that everyone can see them.

Students' arguments typically focus on what happens to the starting amount when the number of pennies in round 10 is doubled. As one student said, "It's like you say 'start, start,' and you're only supposed to have one start."❸

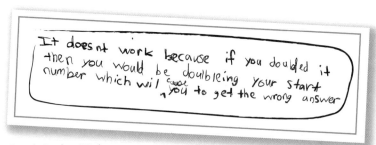

It doesn't work because if you doubled it then you would be doulbleing your start number which wil cause you to get the wrong answer

Sample Student Work

No because 65 doubled is 130 not 125 because it has the starting of 5 in there.

Sample Student Work

Ask follow-up questions such as the following:

- Where is the starting amount in your representation? What happens when you double the amount?

- If we drew this representation for round 10 twice, would we have the number of pennies for round 20? Explain.

- Where is the starting amount in your mathematical expression for round 10? What happens when you double your mathematical expression?

- Can you think of a Penny Jar situation in which doubling the number of pennies in round 10 *does* give you the number of pennies in round 20? Why does it work in that situation but not in this one?

Students may notice that for one of the Penny Jar situations (Start with 0 pennies/Add 8 each round), doubling in this way does work because the start amount is 0.

SESSION FOLLOW-UP
③ Daily Practice and Homework

 Daily Practice: For reinforcement of this unit's content, have students complete *Student Activity Book* page 23.

 Homework: For a review of multiplication, have students complete *Student Activity Book* page 24.

 Student Math Handbook: Students and families may use *Student Math Handbook* pages 79–80 for reference and review. See pages 163–166 in the back of this unit.

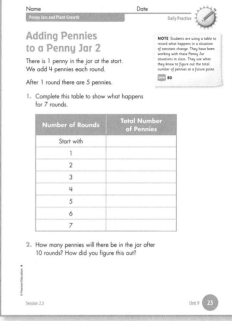

▲ **Student Activity Book, p. 23**

▲ **Student Activity Book, p. 24**

Penny Jar Graphs

Math Focus Points

◈ Identifying points in a graph with corresponding values in a table and interpreting the numerical information in terms of the situation the graph represents

◈ Plotting points on a coordinate grid to represent a situation in which one quantity is changing in relation to another

◈ Making rules that relate one variable to another in situations of constant change

◈ Using symbolic letter notation to represent the value of one variable in terms of another

Today's Plan		Materials
DISCUSSION **①** **Matching Tables and Graphs**	15 MIN · CLASS · PAIRS	• *Student Activity Book,* pp. 25–26 • M23*; T97 • Scissors; glue or tape
ACTIVITY **②** **Making Graphs**	25 MIN · PAIRS · GROUPS	• *Student Activity Book,* pp. 27–28 • M19 (from Session 2.1) • Grid paper*
DISCUSSION **③** **Making Rules**	20 MIN · CLASS	• *Student Activity Book,* p. 28 • T98
SESSION FOLLOW-UP **④** **Daily Practice and Homework**		• *Student Activity Book,* pp. 29–31 • *Student Math Handbook,* pp. 81, 86

*See *Materials to Prepare,* p. 43.

Ten-Minute Math

Closest Estimate Show Problems 7, 8, and 9 on *Closest Estimate* (T91) one at a time. Give students approximately 30 seconds to look at the three possible estimates that are provided and determine which is closest to the actual answer. Have two or three students explain their reasoning for each problem.

How did you break the numbers apart?

How did you determine the magnitude of your answer?

If you changed the numbers in the problem, how did you change them, and why?

Is the closest estimate greater than or less than the actual answer?

How do you know?

DISCUSSION

1 Matching Tables and Graphs

15 MIN   CLASS   PAIRS

Math Focus Points for Discussion

◆ Identifying points in a graph with corresponding values in a table and interpreting the numerical information in terms of the situation the graph represents

Distribute to each student a copy of Penny Jar Tables A and B (M23), which shows two Penny Jar situations: one that starts with 1 penny and increases by 3 pennies, and one that starts with 5 pennies and increases by 2 pennies.

• What can you say about the Penny Jar situation for Table A? How many pennies are there to start with? What will happen as more rounds occur? How many pennies will there be after 10 rounds? How do you know? What about Table B?

• What calculations would you use to find the total number of pennies after 10 rounds?

Show students Penny Jar Graphs 1 and 2 (T97), which also appear in the *Student Activity Book* on pages 25 and 26. Ask students to talk in pairs about the following questions:

One of these graphs represents Table A. The other represents Table B. Which graph goes with which table? How do you know?

Have students turn to *Student Activity Book* pages 25–26. Give them a few minutes to discuss the question, cut out the tables from the handout, and glue or tape them below the corresponding graphs.

Students connect each table with the graph that depicts its data.

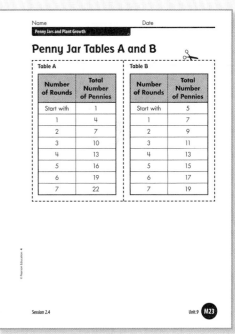

Penny Jars and Plant Growth

Closest Estimate (page 2 of 4)

7. 12)611 ≈	40	50	60
8. 32 × 300 ≈	600	6,200	9,000
9. 525 ÷ 25 ≈	5	20	50
10. 72)648 ≈	10	20	100
11. 41 × 19 ≈	60	80	800
12. 680 ÷ 17 ≈	20	30	40

T91

▲ **Transparencies, T91**

Name _____   Date _____

Penny Jars and Plant Growth

Penny Jar Tables A and B

Table A

Number of Rounds	Total Number of Pennies
Start with	1
1	4
2	7
3	10
4	13
5	16
6	19
7	22

Table B

Number of Rounds	Total Number of Pennies
Start with	5
1	7
2	9
3	11
4	13
5	15
6	17
7	19

Session 2.4   Unit 9 M23

▲ **Resource Masters, M23**

Teaching Note

① Graphing Discrete Values Because there can only be whole numbers of rounds and whole numbers of pennies in the Penny Jar, we use dots on the graph to show the total pennies after each round. You can use a light line to "connect the dots" to help students visualize how the total increases, but keep in mind that there are no actual values between points (i.e., there is no round 4.5, and there are never 6.5 pennies in the jar). See the section on line graphs in the **Teacher Note,** Representing a Constant Rate of Change, p. 140 for further information.

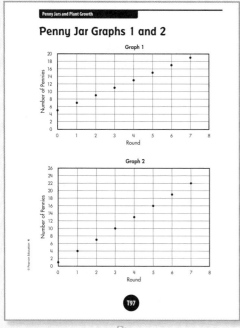

▲ Transparencies, T97

If students are having difficulty reading the graphs, pick a particular point on a graph and ask students what it shows:①

- Put your finger on this point. Which round is it? How many pennies are there?

- Can you find the point that shows round (3)? How can you tell how many pennies there are in round (3)?

- Can you find the point that shows (15) pennies? How can you tell which round that is?

After students have pasted their tables, ask them to describe how they know which table goes with which graph. Use these follow-up questions as needed:

Can you see where the starting amount of pennies is on the table? On the graph? How can you tell what the amount of pennies added each day is when you look at the table? At the graph?

ACTIVITY

② Making Graphs

25 MIN   PAIRS   GROUPS

In this activity, students make a table and a graph for a Penny Jar situation. Each student needs *Student Activity Book* pages 27–28 and a card from Penny Jar Situation Cards (M19). Students can work in pairs but should complete their own tables and graphs.

As you circulate, note the ways that students are writing the expressions for round 100 and choose one or two students to share their methods for the next discussion.

As student pairs finish, organize them into groups of four and have each pair exchange graphs. Ask the students to look at each others' graphs and determine the Penny Jar situation.

Students exchange completed graphs and determine each other's Penny Jar situations.

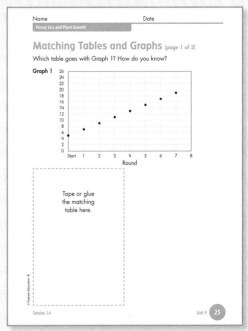

ONGOING ASSESSMENT: Observing Students at Work

Students complete a table for their Penny Jar situation and then graph that situation.

- **Can students represent their Penny Jar situation with a table and a graph?**

- **Do students know how to plot the values on their graph?**

- **Can students determine an arithmetic expression for round 100?**

- **What ideas do students have about why the points fall in a straight line?**

As students are making their graphs, check in with them to see whether they understand the meaning of particular points on the graph. When students have several points on their graphs, ask them what they notice about how the points are arranged. Do they think the points will continue to fall along a straight line? Why do they think that is happening?

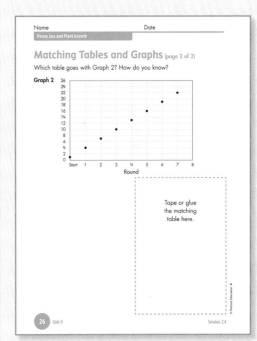

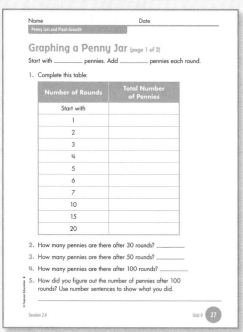

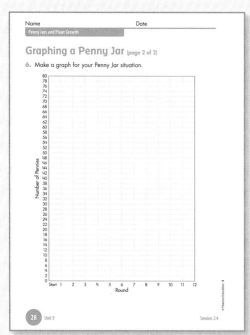

▲ Student Activity Book, p. 27

▲ Student Activity Book, p. 28

DIFFERENTIATION: Supporting the Range of Learners

Intervention Provide students with support by encouraging them to first visualize their Penny Jar situation and then relate that situation to the table and to the graph. While referring to the representations that have been posted in the room, ask questions such as the following:

If you're starting with 3 and adding 4 each day, what would the jar look like after the first round? Where is that amount in your table? Where is it on the graph?

Extension Some students may be interested in graphing Penny Jar situations with higher numbers (e.g., Start with 50/Add 25 each round). In order to do this, they will have to think about what scale they will need to use on their graph. Help them set up appropriate values on their axes on grid paper. Students may want to use calculators to do the actual calculation with large numbers.

DISCUSSION

③ Making Rules

20 MIN   CLASS

Math Focus Points for Discussion

◆ Identifying points in a graph with corresponding values in a table and interpreting the numerical information in terms of the situation the graph represents

◆ Making rules that relate one variable to another in situations of constant change

◆ Using symbolic letter notation to represent the value of one variable in terms of another

You may want to start this discussion by asking students whether they found anything difficult or confusing about making these graphs.

How are these graphs similar to or different from the graphs of temperature and speed that you discussed in Investigation 1? What did you notice about these new graphs?

Students might say:

"These graphs don't have any bends in them."

"Even if you keep going, the Penny Jar graphs would keep going straight."

Steve, you said that you think if you kept going and put more points on the graph, they would still fall in a straight line. Why is that?❷ Why are these graphs straight while the ones about temperature and speed were not straight?

Students may also point out that the number of rounds they could graph on *Student Activity Book* page 28 depended on which Penny Jar Situation Card they graphed. If students mention this, ask them why this is true. Re-create their graph using Blank Penny Jar Graph (T98).

Students might say:

"I did a Penny Jar graph that started with 4 pennies in the jar and I added 9 pennies every day. I could only go up to round 8 on my graph. But other people were able to go to round 12."

Does anybody have any ideas about why this is true?

After students have shared their ideas about why these graphs are straight, ask them about their arithmetic expressions for round 100. Have one or two students explain their methods.

Students might say:

"Multiply 100 by 2 and then add 9."

"It's 9 + 2 + 2 + 2 + 2 + 2 . . . a hundred times."

Math Note

❷ **Constant Change** In Investigation 1, students encountered graphs of temperature and speed. In these graphs, the amount of change was not constant. For example, from one week to the next on a temperature graph, the temperature may go up or down by any amount. The Penny Jar is a situation of constant change. The same number of pennies is added each day. For any amount of change on the *x*-axis, the change on the *y*-axis is the same, resulting in a straight line. Students may talk about how the "steepness" or "slantiness" of the line will not change because the amount of increase is always the same.

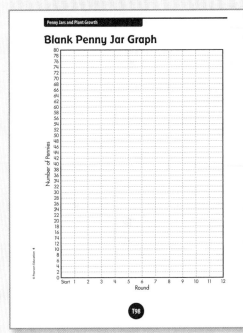

▲ Transparencies, T98

Math Note

❸ **Ratio Relationships** Some students may notice that the rule for the Penny Jar situation "Start with 0 pennies/Add 8 each round" looks somewhat different from the others. For example, a student might say, "You can just multiply by 8 because you just add 8 each time and you didn't have any pennies in the jar at the beginning, so my rule is 'the round number times 8.'" Other students may think of the rule as "0 plus 8 times the round number." In this Penny Jar situation, unlike the others, there is a ratio relationship between number of rounds and number of pennies.

Teaching Note

❹ **Choosing Variables** Some students may suggest using more than one letter, such as, *nr*, for "number of rounds." If so, tell them that mathematicians use a single letter to stand for "any number" of something, and so they need to choose only one letter. It can be any letter they choose, although mathematicians often use *n* or *x*. (Note that in standard notation *nr* could actually mean $n \times r$, but you need not introduce this notation with students.) Let students know that this discussion is an introduction. Some students will need more examples before they are successful at making rules, either with words or with symbols. Students will do more work with rule-writing in the remaining sessions of this Investigation.

Record what the student says in written language and then as an arithmetic expression: $(100 \times 2) + 9$.

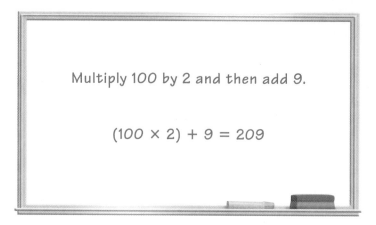

Multiply 100 by 2 and then add 9.

$(100 \times 2) + 9 = 209$

Ask questions to connect the expression with the situation:

What does the 100 mean? Why is it multiplied by 2? Why is the 9 added?

How could you change this expression so that it would tell you the number for 200 rounds or 300 rounds?

Once these are recorded as $(200 \times 2) + 9$ and $(300 \times 2) + 9$, talk about a rule for finding the number of pennies for any round. Write students' ideas for these rules in their words. For example:

I'm going to write what Amelia said: Multiply the number of rounds by 2. Then add 9.❸

Write these words as an arithmetic expression and introduce the idea of using a letter as a symbol for "number of rounds":

I could write Amelia's rule like this: (Number of rounds $\times 2$) + 9. Mathematicians often use letters to write rules like this one. What letter do you want to use for "number of rounds"?

Students might suggest using *r* or *n* for the number of rounds.❹ Have students help you use this symbol to write an expression for the rule. For example: $(n \times 2) + 9$ or $9 + (r \times 2)$.

Invite students to look at the expression they wrote for round 100, and suggest that they now write a rule that applies for any round. They can write the rule in words or as an expression using symbols.

SESSION FOLLOW-UP
Daily Practice and Homework

 Daily Practice: For ongoing review, have students complete *Student Activity Book* page 29.

 Homework: Students complete Penny Jar tables with missing values and determine the number of pennies in rounds 10 and 20 on *Student Activity Book* pages 30–31.

 Student Math Handbook: Students and families may use *Student Math Handbook* pages 81 and 86 for reference and review. See pages 163–166 in the back of this unit.

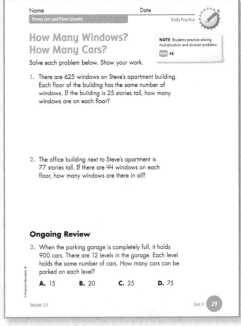

▲ **Student Activity Book, p. 29**

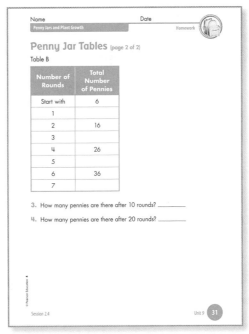

▲ **Student Activity Book, p. 31**

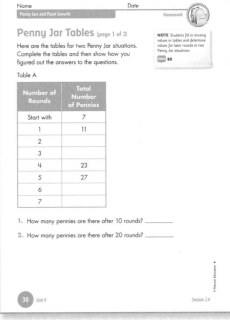

▲ **Student Activity Book, p. 30**

Assessment: Penny Jar Comparisons

Math Focus Points

◆ Finding the value of one quantity in a situation of constant change, given the value of the other

◆ Writing an arithmetic expression for finding the value of one quantity in terms of the other in a situation of constant change

◆ Comparing situations by describing the differences in their graphs

Today's Plan		Materials
1 **ACTIVITY** **Introducing Windows and Towers**	15 MIN CLASS	• Connecting cubes; chart paper*
2 **MATH WORKSHOP** **Penny Jars and Towers** **2A** Windows and Towers **2B** Assessment: Penny Jar Comparisons	45 MIN	**2A** • *Student Activity Book*, pp. 33–34 • Connecting cubes **2B** • *Student Activity Book*, pp. 35–37 • M26*; M27* ☑
3 **SESSION FOLLOW-UP** **Daily Practice and Homework**		• *Student Activity Book*, pp. 38–39 • *Student Math Handbook*, pp. 82–85

*See *Materials to Prepare*, p. 43.

Ten-Minute Math

Closest Estimate Show Problems 10, 11, and 12 on *Closest Estimate* (T91) one at a time. Give students approximately 30 seconds to look at the three possible estimates that are provided and to determine which is closest to the actual answer. Have two or three students explain their reasoning for each problem.

How did you break the numbers apart?

How did you determine the magnitude of your answer?

If you changed the numbers in the problem, how did you change them, and why?

Is the closest estimate greater than or less than the actual answer?

How do you know?

ACTIVITY

15 MIN CLASS

Introducing Windows and Towers

Distribute 10 to 12 connecting cubes to each student. Then introduce the Windows and Towers activity by having students build the first few floors of a single tower and then of a double tower. Start by holding up one connecting cube.

This is called a *single tower,* one floor high. Each side of the tower has a window, and there is a skylight on the top. It has 5 windows total. Skylights count as windows.

Now take another cube to make a tower two floors high. Have students build the same tower, and ask how many windows are on this tower. Since the face of each cube has 1 window and there are 4 windows facing out for each of the two floors and 1 skylight at the top, there are 9 windows total.

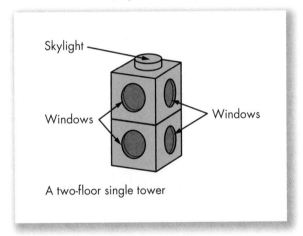

Skylight

Windows

Windows

A two-floor single tower

Add another cube or two and focus on what happens to the skylight.

How many skylights are there when there are three floors? Does this change as we add on more floors?

Establish with students that the number of skylights is the same; there is always 1 skylight on the single tower. Post the prepared table on chart paper, and begin recording the number of windows on each floor of the single tower. As a class, complete the table for the first 10 floors of a single tower.

Number of floors	Number of windows
1	5
2	9
3	13
4	17
5	21
6	25
7	29
8	33
9	37
10	41

Introduce a *double tower,* a tower with two cubes on each "floor," by showing a double tower with one floor. Make sure that students understand how to count the number of windows (6) and the number of skylights (2). Then add one more floor.

How many windows, including skylights, are there now? How do you know?

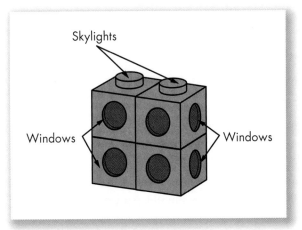

Skylights

Windows   Windows

Students might say:

 "14. I counted every window and skylight."

 "14. There are 6 windows for each floor and 2 skylights: (6 × 2) + 2 = 12 + 2 = 14."

 "14. The top floor has 8 windows including the skylights. Then I added on 6 windows for each additional floor: 8 + 6 = 14."

MATH WORKSHOP

45 MIN

2 Penny Jars and Towers

In this Math Workshop, which continues in the next two sessions, students work on two activities, Windows and Towers, and Penny Jar Comparisons. These activities focus on representing situations of constant change with tables, arithmetic expressions, and graphs, They also focus on describing one value (e.g., the number of pennies) in terms of another value (e.g., the number of rounds).

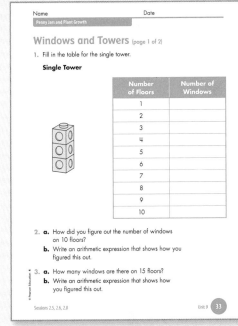

Name _____ Date _____

Penny Jars and Plant Growth

Windows and Towers (page 1 of 2)

1. Fill in the table for the single tower.

Single Tower

Number of Floors	Number of Windows
1	
2	
3	
4	
5	
6	
7	
8	
9	
10	

2. **a.** How did you figure out the number of windows on 10 floors?
   b. Write an arithmetic expression that shows how you figured this out.

3. **a.** How many windows are there on 15 floors?
   b. Write an arithmetic expression that shows how you figured this out.

Sessions 2.5, 2.6, 2.8   Unit 9 33

▲ **Student Activity Book, p. 33**

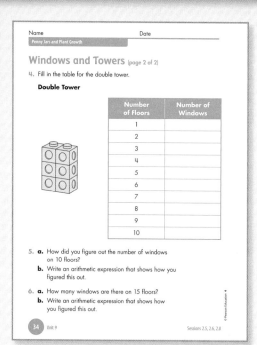

Student Activity Book, p. 34

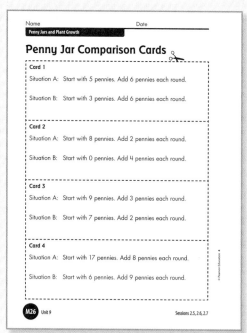

Resource Masters, M26

You will be assessing students' work on one of the Penny Jar Comparison problems (Card 1). Plan to have some students work on the assessment activity while others work on Windows and Towers problems, so that you have the opportunity to observe each pair of students for the assessment.

2A Windows and Towers

PAIRS

Distribute 50 connecting cubes to each pair of students. In this activity, students build single and double towers. For each tower, they determine the number of windows, including skylights, for towers that are one floor, two floors, three floors, and so on, up to 10 floors high. They record this information on *Student Activity Book* pages 33–34, in a table for each kind of tower. Finally, students write arithmetic expressions for the number of windows for 10- and 15-floor towers.

Students determine the total number of windows for multi-floor single and double towers.

ONGOING ASSESSMENT: Observing Students at Work

Students complete a table of values for both the single and double towers and answer questions about the total number of windows for 10 and 15 floors.

- **Do students correctly determine the number of windows and skylights on the towers?**

- **Do students fill in the tables by adding the same amount each time?**

- **Do students write arithmetic expressions that correctly represent the number of windows?**

- **Do students use multiplication to show how the number of windows is related to the number of floors?**

- **Do students begin to articulate a general rule for finding the number of windows?**

As you work with students, ask them to explain how the numbers in their tables are connected to the cube structures and to any arithmetic they may have used.

What does this row in your table show? What does the 7 mean? What does the 29 mean? Show me the 29 windows on your single tower for the 7 floors. How many are skylights? Why are you multiplying 7 by 4?

Some students may begin to talk about a general rule for finding the number of windows for any number of floors. Encourage students to jot down their ideas. They will work on rules for the towers in Session 2.8.

DIFFERENTIATION: Supporting the Range of Learners

Intervention Students who have difficulty keeping track of the number of windows may find it useful to write out the arithmetic expression for the number of windows on each successive floor (e.g., 5, 5 + 4, 5 + 4 + 4, 5 + 4 + 4 + 4, and so on). Seeing this series of arithmetic expressions and matching each number to what it represents in the towers may also help students create their own arithmetic expressions for 10 and 15 floors.

Extension Students who need a challenge can be asked how to determine the number of windows for 30, 40, or 50 floors. Challenge these students to write a general rule for finding the number of windows for any number of floors.

2B Assessment: Penny Jar Comparisons

PAIRS

In this activity, students use *Student Activity Book* pages 35–37, plus a copy of Card 1 from Penny Jar Comparison Cards (M26), to compare the number of pennies accumulated in two different Penny Jars. Penny Jar Situation A begins with more pennies than Penny Jar Situation B. Students consider whether Penny Jar Situation B will ever catch up with Penny Jar Situation A and explain why.

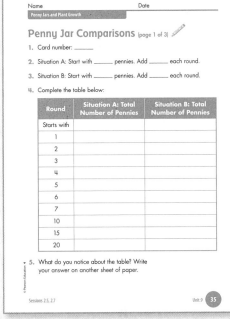

▲ Student Activity Book, p. 35; Resource Masters, M28

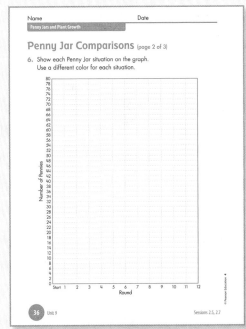

▲ Student Activity Book, p. 36; Resource Masters, M29

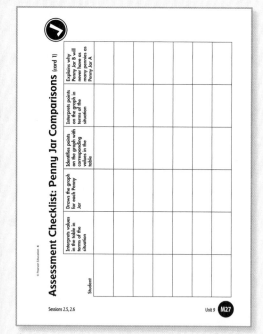

▲ **Student Activity Book, p. 37;**
Resource Masters, M30

▲ **Resource Masters, M27**

Use students' work on Card 1 only as an assessment of how well students are making sense of tables and graphs. This assessment focuses on three of the unit's benchmarks: Benchmark 1: Connect tables and graphs to each other and to the situations they represent; Benchmark 2: Make a graph on a coordinate grid from a table of values; and Benchmark 4: Take into account the starting amount and the amount of change in describing and comparing situations of constant change.

You can learn the most from this assessment if you question students while they are working on Card 1, and if you also inspect the completed copies of their *Student Activity Book* pages. You can use Assessment Checklist: Penny Jar Comparisons (M27) to record your notes on each student.

If you do not have time to observe all students' work on Card 1 during this session, complete this assessment during Math Workshop in Session 2.6.

On their written work, look at questions 5, 7, and 8, in which they write what they notice about the table and the graph and explain why Penny Jar B (Start with 3 pennies/Add 6 each round) will never have as many pennies as Penny Jar A (Start with 5 pennies/Add 6 each round). Do they notice that the table shows a constant increase by 6 for both Penny Jar situations? Do they describe how the points on the graph fall on a straight line and how that shows that the same number of pennies is added each day? Can they explain why Penny Jar B will never have as many pennies as Penny Jar A?

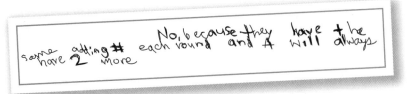

Sample Student Work

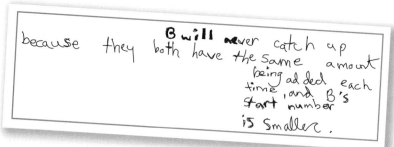

Sample Student Work

If needed upon examination of their writing, follow up with individual students to help clarify their understanding of the table and the graph.

ONGOING ASSESSMENT: Observing Students at Work

Students compare tables and graphs of two Penny Jar situations.

- **Do students explain how values in the table are related to the Penny Jar situations?**

- **Do students graph the two Penny Jar situations accurately?**

- **Do students explain how points on the graph are related to the Penny Jar situations?**

- **Do students use the starting amounts and the amount added each round to determine that Penny Jar B will never have as many pennies as Penny Jar A?**

As students are working, ask questions to determine whether they are bringing meaning to the table and to the graph:

- What does this row of the table mean? (Point to a row of the table.) What does the (6) mean? What does the (41) mean? Where can you find the same information on your graph?

- What does this point mean? (Select a point on the graph.) Where can you find the same information in your table?

SESSION FOLLOW-UP

③ Daily Practice and Homework

 Daily Practice: For ongoing review, have students complete *Student Activity Book* page 38.

 Homework: Students create a Penny Jar situation of their own using *Student Activity Book* page 39. Encourage students to choose numbers that are not too easy or too difficult for them.

 Student Math Handbook: Students and families may use *Student Math Handbook* pages 82–85 for reference and review. See pages 163–166 in the back of this unit.

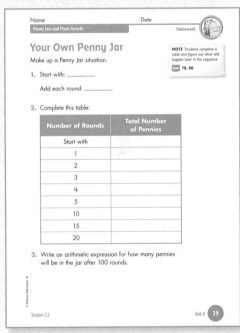

▲ **Student Activity Book, p. 38**

▲ **Student Activity Book, p. 39**

Can There Be 15 Windows?

Math Focus Points

◆ Finding the value of one quantity in a situation of constant change, given the value of the other

◆ Writing an arithmetic expression for finding the value of one quantity in terms of the other in a situation of constant change

◆ Comparing situations by describing the differences in their graphs

Today's Plan		Materials
① DISCUSSION **Single and Double Towers**	20 MIN CLASS	• *Student Activity Book,* pp. 33–34 (from Session 2.5) • Connecting cubes
② MATH WORKSHOP **Penny Jars and Towers** **②A** Backward Problems for Single and Double Towers **②B** Windows on Square and Corner Towers **②C** Penny Jar Comparisons	40 MIN	**②A** • *Student Activity Book,* pp. 41–42 • Connecting cubes **②B** • *Student Activity Book,* pp. 43–46 • Connecting cubes **②C** • *Student Activity Book,* pp. 35–37 (optional) • M26 (from Session 2.5); M27 (optional); M28–M30*
③ SESSION FOLLOW-UP **Daily Practice and Homework**		• *Student Activity Book,* pp. 47–48 • *Student Math Handbook,* pp. 80–81

*See *Materials to Prepare,* p. 45.

Ten-Minute Math

Closest Estimate Show Problems 13, 14, and 15 on *Closest Estimate* (T92) one at a time. Give students approximately 30 seconds to look at the three possible estimates that are provided and to determine which is closest to the actual answer. Have two or three students explain their reasoning for each problem.

- How did you break the numbers apart?
- How did you determine the magnitude of your answer?
- If you changed the numbers in the problem, how did you change them, and why?
- Is the closest estimate greater than or less than the actual answer?
- How do you know?

① Single and Double Towers

20 MIN   CLASS

Math Focus Points for Discussion

◆ Finding the value of one quantity in a situation of constant change, given the value of the other

Students come to this discussion with their work on *Student Activity Book* pages 33–34. They should also have cubes available to demonstrate their ideas.

Begin by asking what the tables show about how the number of windows on each tower increases. For example, for the single tower, in which the numbers start with 5 and go up by 4 (5, 9, 13, 17, 21, . . .), you might ask:

What does the 4 stand for? How do you see 5 in the cube tower? Show us where the 17 windows are in the four-floor tower. How many skylights are there?

Ask similar questions for the double towers as well. Students' explanations might approach rules for the number of windows in a tower.

Students might say:

"You get the number of windows by skip counting by 4s, starting at 5."

"You get the number of windows by multiplying the number of floors by 4 and then adding the window on the top of the building."

Now pose a problem (called a "backward problem" in this Investigation) that asks students to determine whether a tower can ever have a specific number of windows:

Can a single tower ever have exactly 50 windows?

Give students a few minutes to consider this question in pairs, and then bring them together again to share ideas. Some students may observe that the number of windows on a single tower is always odd, so it cannot have 50 windows. Have them explain why it works out that there are only odd numbers. Other students may say that the number always has to be 1 more than a multiple of 4. Ask them to explain their reasoning by referring to the tower.

Penny Jars and Plant Growth

Closest Estimate (page 3 of 4)

13. $225 \times 18 \approx$	2,250	3,500	4,000
14. $11\overline{)561} \approx$	15	50	60
15. $900 \div 27 \approx$	30	40	50
16. $422 \div 13 \approx$	30	40	50
17. $88 \times 59 \approx$	4,800	5,000	5,400
18. $32\overline{)912} \approx$	30	80	100

T92

▲ Transparencies, T92

Is there a single tower with exactly 51 windows—and, if so, how many floors does it have?

Some students may think that there can be a single tower with 51 windows, because 51 is an odd number. Others may say that because there are 4 windows on each floor plus 1 skylight, we know that there has to be 4 times some number plus 1, and try to find a value for which this works. Others may add on by 4s to the last known number of windows to determine whether a single tower can have 51 windows.

At the end of the discussion, introduce two additional towers: square towers and corner towers. Square towers are built from 4 cubes arranged as a square for each floor. Corner towers are built from 3 cubes arranged as a corner or "L" for each floor. With each new tower, establish with students the number of windows on each floor and the number of skylights on each building. The square tower has 8 windows on each floor and 4 skylights. The corner tower has 8 windows on each floor and 3 skylights.

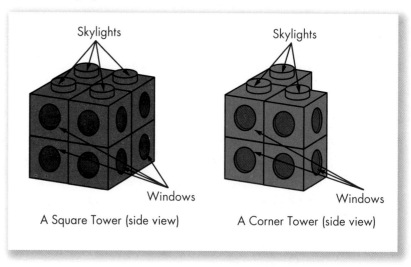

A Square Tower (side view)   A Corner Tower (side view)

MATH WORKSHOP

40 MIN

② Penny Jars and Towers

In Math Workshop, students continue to work on Penny Jar Comparisons, and on more Windows and Towers problems (Backward Problems for Single and Double Towers, and Windows on Square and Corner Towers).

By the end of the Math Workshop in the next session, all students should finish Penny Jar Comparison Cards 2–3.

2A Backward Problems for Single and Double Towers

PAIRS

In this activity, students solve backward problems for single and double towers and explain their solutions on *Student Activity Book* pages 41–42. Some students may build the towers; others may reason from tables or from arithmetic sentences expressing the number of windows based on the number of floors. Make available 50 connecting cubes per pair.

As you circulate, note the strategies students use to determine whether a given number of windows is possible for a single or double tower.

ONGOING ASSESSMENT: Observing Students at Work

Students determine whether single and double towers can ever have a given number of windows.

- **Do students correctly determine the number of windows and the number of skylights on the towers?**

- **Are students able to determine whether a tower will have exactly a given number of windows?** If so, do they determine the number of floors?

Students use number relationships including factors and multiples to solve the backward problems for a double tower.

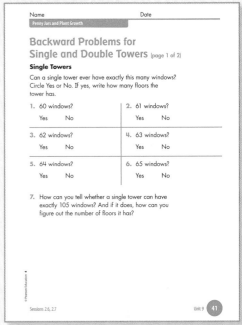

Name _____ Date _____

Penny Jars and Plant Growth

Backward Problems for
Single and Double Towers (page 1 of 2)

Single Towers

Can a single tower ever have exactly this many windows? Circle Yes or No. If yes, write how many floors the tower has.

1. 60 windows?   2. 61 windows?
   Yes   No   Yes   No

3. 62 windows?   4. 63 windows?
   Yes   No   Yes   No

5. 64 windows?   6. 65 windows?
   Yes   No   Yes   No

7. How can you tell whether a single tower can have exactly 105 windows? And if it does, how can you figure out the number of floors it has?

Sessions 2.6, 2.7   Unit 9   41

▲ Student Activity Book, p. 41

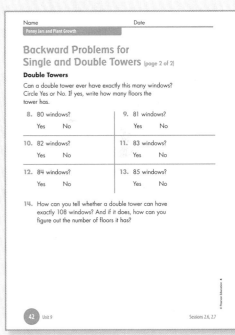

Name _____ Date _____

Penny Jars and Plant Growth

Backward Problems for
Single and Double Towers (page 2 of 2)

Double Towers

Can a double tower ever have exactly this many windows? Circle Yes or No. If yes, write how many floors the tower has.

8. 80 windows?   9. 81 windows?
   Yes   No   Yes   No

10. 82 windows?   11. 83 windows?
    Yes   No   Yes   No

12. 84 windows?   13. 85 windows?
    Yes   No   Yes   No

14. How can you tell whether a double tower can have exactly 108 windows? And if it does, how can you figure out the number of floors it has?

42 Unit 9   Sessions 2.6, 2.7

▲ Student Activity Book, p. 42

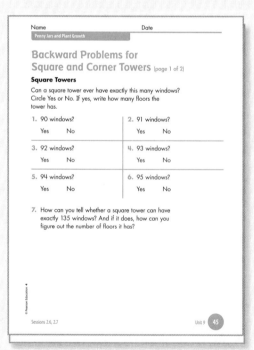

▲ Student Activity Book, pp. 43–44

▲ Student Activity Book, pp. 45–46

DIFFERENTIATION: Supporting the Range of Learners

Intervention If students are unable to work with the numbers given on the *Student Activity Book* pages, suggest smaller numbers. After solving some of the problems by building and counting, give students another possible number of windows. Ask them to talk through with you whether the tower can have that number, without building the tower first.

2B Windows on Square and Corner Towers

GROUPS

In this activity, students complete *Student Activity Book* pages 43–44 and pages 45–46, both relating to square and corner towers. First they list the number of windows as the number of floors increases from 1 to 10 and answer questions about larger numbers of floors. Then, they solve backward problems to determine whether a given number of windows is possible for a given kind of tower. Make available 50 connecting cubes per group.

ONGOING ASSESSMENT: Observing Students at Work

Students complete tables for corner and square towers, write arithmetic expressions for the number of windows for particular numbers of floors, and determine whether they can ever have a given number of windows for a particular tower.

- **Do students correctly determine the number of windows and skylights on the towers?**

- **Can students write arithmetic expressions that represent the number of windows for a particular number of floors?**

- **Are students able to determine whether a tower will have exactly a given number of windows?**

- **If a tower has a given number of windows, can students determine the number of floors?**

DIFFERENTIATION: Supporting the Range of Learners

Extension For students who are figuring out the number of windows easily, you can provide more challenging numbers in the blank spaces in the tables on *Student Activity Book* pages 43–44.

2C Penny Jar Comparisons

PAIRS

For an overview of this activity, see Session 2.5, pages 81–82. ➊

Distribute a set of Penny Jar Comparison Cards (M26) and copies of Penny Jar Comparisons (M28–M30) to students. Students should work on Cards 2 and 3 first, in either order. Card 4 presents a more difficult problem.

ONGOING ASSESSMENT: Observing Students at Work

Students make a table and a graph to compare two Penny Jar situations and answer questions about what they notice.

- **Can students complete the table and graph for each Penny Jar situation?**

- **Can students calculate the number of pennies for rounds 10, 15, and 20?**

- **Do students correctly determine whether situation B ever catches up to situation A?**

- **What do students use to explain their conclusions?** What do they notice from the tables? What do they notice from the graphs?

Encourage students to refer to their tables and graphs in their explanations comparing Penny Jar situations A and B.

As students are working, ask them questions that focus on comparing the way the total number of pennies is increasing.

- (For Card 2) What happens from round 1 to round 4? What does your graph show for round 4? What does it mean that the dots on your graph are in the same place for Penny Jar A and Penny Jar B for round 4? What happens after round 4? What do you think will happen if we keep putting pennies in the jar for more rounds after round 12?

- (For Card 3) What happens to your two graphs as more and more rounds of pennies are put in the jars? Do you think Penny Jar B will ever have more pennies than Penny Jar A? Why? What do you think will happen if we keep putting pennies in the jar for more rounds after round 12?

- (For Card 4) What happens from round 1 to round 6? How do the two graphs compare? What happens from round 10 to 12? What do you think will happen after round 12? Why?

Teaching Note

➊ **Assessment** If you did not complete your assessment of students' work on Penny Jar Comparision Card 1 in the previous session, continue your observations with the Assessment Checklist (M27) during this Math Workshop.

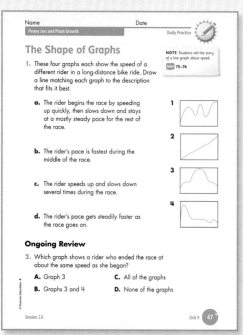

▲ Student Activity Book, p. 47

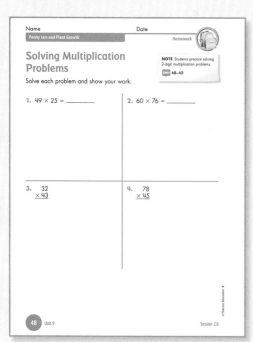

▲ Student Activity Book, p. 48

DIFFERENTIATION: Supporting the Range of Learners

Intervention Some students may need continued support in graphing the two Penny Jar situations. Help students relate the point on the graph to the corresponding values in the table and to the Penny Jar situation. You can also demonstrate putting one or two points on the graph.

SESSION FOLLOW-UP

③ Daily Practice and Homework

Daily Practice: For reinforcement of this unit's content, have students complete *Student Activity Book* page 47.

Homework: For a review of multiplication, have students complete *Student Activity Book* page 48.

Student Math Handbook: Students and families may use *Student Math Handbook* pages 80–81 for reference and review. See pages 163–166 in the back of this unit.

Comparing Penny Jar Situations

Math Focus Points

◆ Describing the relative steepness of graphs or parts of graphs in terms of different rates of change

◆ Making rules that relate one variable to another in situations of constant change

◆ Using symbolic letter notation to represent the value of one variable in terms of another

Today's Plan		Materials
① MATH WORKSHOP **Penny Jars and Towers** **1A** Backward Problems for Single and Double Towers **1B** Windows on Square and Corner Towers **1C** Penny Jar Comparisons	🕐 35 MIN	**1A** • Materials from Session 2.6 **1B** • Materials from Session 2.6 **1C** • Materials from Session 2.6
② DISCUSSION **Comparing Two Penny Jar Situations**	🕐 25 MIN 👥 CLASS	• *Student Activity Book*, pp. 35–37 • M28–M30; T99–T102*🖨 • Chart paper
③ SESSION FOLLOW-UP **Daily Practice and Homework**		• *Student Activity Book*, pp. 49–51 • *Student Math Handbook*, pp. 82–85

*See *Materials to Prepare*, p. 45.

Ten-Minute Math

Quick Survey   For the survey, ask the class, "What is your favorite season—spring, summer, fall, or winter?" or a different categorical question that you or the students choose. Make sure they collect data about something they already know or can observe easily. With today's data, make a bar graph. Ask students:

• What do you notice about the data?

• What do the data tell us about our class?

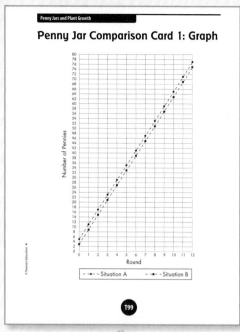

Penny Jars and Plant Growth

Penny Jar Comparison Card 1: Graph

T99

▲ Transparencies, T99

MATH WORKSHOP
① Penny Jars and Towers

35 MIN

In Math Workshop, students continue to work with Windows and Towers and with Penny Jar Comparisons. All students should have completed Penny Jar Comparison Card 1 by now, and should complete Cards 2 and 3 before the discussion at the end of this session. They also need to complete Windows on Square and Corner Towers in preparation for Session 2.8.

ⒶA Backward Problems for Single and Double Towers

PAIRS

For complete details about this activity, see Session 2.6, page 87.

ⒷB Windows on Square and Corner Towers

PAIRS

For complete details about this activity, see Session 2.6, page 88.

ⒸC Penny Jar Comparisons

PAIRS

For complete details about this activity, see Session 2.5, pages 81–82.

DISCUSSION
② Comparing Two Penny Jar Situations

25 MIN CLASS

Math Focus Points for Discussion

◆ Describing the relative steepness of graphs or parts of graphs in terms of different rates of change

◆ Making rules that relate one variable to another in situations of constant change

◆ Using symbolic letter notation to represent the value of one variable in terms of another

This discussion focuses on comparing two Penny Jar situations by looking at the tables and graphs. The graphs are especially helpful for seeing how two situations change at the same rate or how one increases faster than the other. Display the graphs for Penny Jar Comparison Cards 1–3 (T99–T101). Students may describe the graphs using phrases such as "going up faster," or "one is steeper than the other." Some students may articulate ideas about the differences in the constant change represented in the graphs and tables: "Penny Jar B goes up two more than Penny Jar A each time, so Penny Jar B gets closer and closer."

Students come to the discussion with their completed work on *Student Activity Book* pages 35–37 and Penny Jar Comparisons (M28–M30) for Penny Jar Comparison Cards 1–3. Begin the discussion by focusing on Card 1. Invite students to explain their conclusions.

Will Penny Jar B ever catch up? How can you explain what happens?

Students might say:

"Penny Jar A starts with more, and then it gets the same number as B every time. Penny Jar A will always stay ahead."

For Card 1, how does the graph show that Penny Jar B never catches up to Penny Jar A? Where do you see that on the table? How does the graph show that the same number of pennies is added each round for both Jars A and B?

Have two or three students explain and provide opportunities for other students to ask questions. Once the tables and graph for Card 1 are shared and discussed, turn to Cards 2 and 3. Invite students to share their explanations, including their tables and graphs. Students may note that for Card 2, Penny Jar A has more at first, then Penny Jars A and B are the same, and then Penny Jar B has more. Ask questions to connect their conclusions with the tables and with the graph.❶

For Card 2, will Penny Jar B ever catch up? How can you explain what happens? How does the table show this? What do you see when you look at the graph? How is the relationship between the two situations on Card 2 different from what you described about Card 1? How does what happens on Card 3 compare to Cards 1 and 2?

Professional Development

❶ **Dialogue Box:** Comparing Penny Jars, p. 158

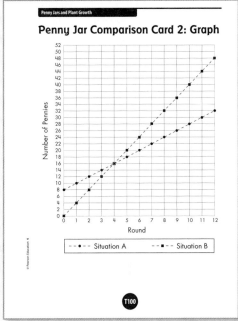

▲ Transparencies, T100

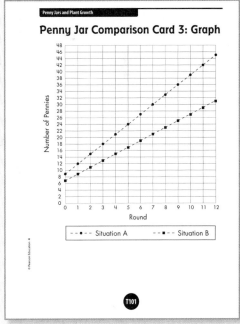

▲ Transparencies, T101

❷ **Catching Up** Some students notice the effects of the difference in the two rates of increase. For example, in describing Penny Jar Comparison Card 2, students say, "It's catching up by 2," and reason that it will take 4 rounds for B to catch up to A since Penny Jar A starts with 8 (or 4 × 2) more pennies.

Encourage students to talk about what the parallel lines of dots for Card 1 show about the two situations (the number of pennies is increasing at the same rate); then what the intersecting lines of dots for Card 2 show (Penny Jar B starts with fewer pennies but increases at a greater rate and eventually has the same number and then more pennies than Penny Jar A).❷ Finally, discuss what the diverging lines of dots for Card 3 show (Penny Jar A starts with more pennies *and* the number increases at a greater rate, so the difference between the number of pennies gets larger and larger).

Conclude the discussion by asking students about rules for one or two of the Penny Jar situations on the cards. Ask them to say in words how they would find the number of pennies for any round—for example, of Penny Jar A on Card 1. Write down students' rules.

Once students have described their rules in words, reintroduce symbolic letter notation for "any number." Ask students if they can think of a way to write the rule using a letter (*n* or *r* or *x*) to stand for the number of rounds as you did in Session 2.4.

If *n* stands for some number of rounds, what do we have to do to that *n* to find the total number of pennies? How did we do it when *n* was 5 rounds? When *n* was 10 rounds?

Students might say:

"I multiplied 10 times 6, because it was 6 pennies for each round. Then I added 5."

"I started with 5, then I knew 6 × 10 = 60, so I added 60."

Record your students' methods as arithmetic expressions. For example:❸

$$(10 \times 6) + 5 \qquad 5 + (6 \times 10)$$

Then ask how students could use the expressions for a particular round as the basis for an expression that works for *any* round:

So how could we use Enrique's method for any number of rounds? Instead of 10 rounds, what symbol could we use to stand for any number of rounds?

Students might say:

"You could use R for the number of rounds. It would be R × 6."

"You still have to add 5 for the pennies you had at the start, so it's R × 6 + 5."

"If you didn't know the start number, you could use a letter for that, too. It could be R × 6 + S."

Test students' expressions by using some specific number of rounds. If time remains, develop a rule and a symbolic expression for one of the other Penny Jar situations on the cards.

If you have additional time and enough of your students worked on Card 4, you can also discuss the graph and rules for the Penny Jar situations on Card 4, Penny Jar Comparison Card 4: Graph (T102). You will have another discussion about developing rules and notation in the next session.

Math Note

❸ **Using Parentheses** In the standard order of operations, multiplication and division are carried out before addition and subtraction. Thus, neither of the expressions listed here *requires* parentheses. However, this is a good opportunity to help students learn the meaning of parentheses in arithmetic expressions—that operations inside the parentheses are carried out before the rest of the expression. Using parentheses in the expression $5 + (6 \times 10)$ helps students see how the expression represents the situation. It matches how students describe their method. It also makes completely clear how the expression should be evaluated: 5 plus the quantity (6×10), *not* the quantity $(5 + 6)$ multiplied by 10.

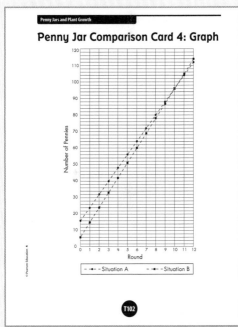

▲ Transparencies, T102

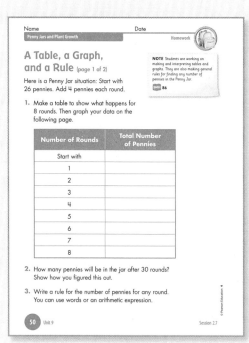

▲ **Student Activity Book, p. 49**

SESSION FOLLOW-UP

3 Daily Practice and Homework

 Daily Practice: For ongoing review, have students complete *Student Activity Book* page 49.

Homework: Using *Student Activity Book* pages 50–51, students practice making a table and a graph. They also create a rule for a Penny Jar situation using either words or notations.

Student Math Handbook: Students and families may use *Student Math Handbook* pages 82–85 for reference and review. See pages 163–166 in the back of this unit.

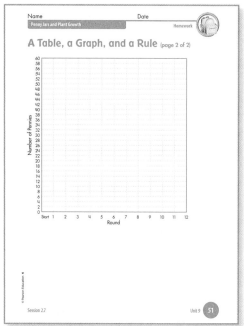

▲ **Student Activity Book, p. 51**

▲ **Student Activity Book, p. 50**

Rules for Windows and Towers

Math Focus Points

◆ Making rules that relate one variable to another in situations of constant change

◆ Using symbolic letter notation to represent the value of one variable in terms of another

Today's Plan		Materials
① ACTIVITY **Finding Rules**	🕐 👤 👥 **35 MIN** **PAIRS** **GROUPS**	• *Student Activity Book*, pp. 33–34 (from Session 2.5); *Student Activity Book*, pp. 43–44 (from Session 2.7); 53–54 • Connecting cubes; chart paper*; grid paper
② DISCUSSION **Rules for Towers**	🕐 👥 **25 MIN** **CLASS**	• *Student Activity Book*, pp. 53–54
③ SESSION FOLLOW-UP **Daily Practice and Homework**		• *Student Activity Book*, pp. 55–57 • *Student Math Handbook*, p. 86

*See *Materials to Prepare*, p. 45.

Ten-Minute Math

Closest Estimate Show Problems 16, 17, and 18 on *Closest Estimate* (T92) one at a time. Give students approximately 30 seconds to look at the three possible estimates that are provided and to determine which is closest to the actual answer. Have two or three students explain their reasoning for each problem.

How did you break the numbers apart?

How did you determine the magnitude of your answer?

If you changed the numbers in the problem, how did you change them, and why?

Is the closest estimate greater than or less than the actual answer?

How do you know?

35 MIN   PAIRS   GROUPS

ACTIVITY

1 Finding Rules

In this activity, students use their finished tables from *Student Activity Book* pages 33–34 and 43–44 to write rules for finding the number of windows on towers of any kind and for any number of floors.

Begin this activity with a brief discussion of the single tower.

Sketch a table for a single tower using the three-column format introduced in Session 2.3 for Penny Jars. As a whole group, fill in the first few entries:

Single Tower

Number of floors	Calculation	Total number of windows
1	1 + 4	5
2	1 + 4 + 4 5 + 4 (2 × 4) + 1	9
3	5 + (2 × 4) 1 + 4 + 4 + 4 (3 × 4) + 1	13
4		
5		
6		
7		
8		
9		
10		

Ask students to explain each entry and how the numbers are connected to the number of floors.

Students might say:

"If it is 3 floors, then you add the 4 three times."

"For the third floor, you multiply 3 by 4, and then add 1 for the skylight."

What arithmetic expression will tell how many windows there are for a single tower that is 100 floors high?

Some students may say $(100 \times 4) + 1$. Others may say $1 + 4 + 4 + 4 + 4 + \ldots + 4$ (100 times). Have students explain their reasoning.

Remind students about letter notation, and ask them how they can represent a rule for a single tower using n (or some other letter).

Do you remember that we talked about how you can use n to stand for any number when making a rule? How can we write a rule that uses n to stand for any number?

Help students use their notation for 100 floors to come up with an expression using n. For example: $(n \times 4) + 1$ or $1 + (n \times 4)$. Ask students how they could use this expression to find the number of windows in 200 floors.

After this introduction, provide pairs or small groups of students with 50 connecting cubes each as they work on *Student Activity Book* pages 53 and 54. Draw students' attention to the four prepared charts. As groups find a rule for a certain kind of tower, they write their rule on the appropriate chart.

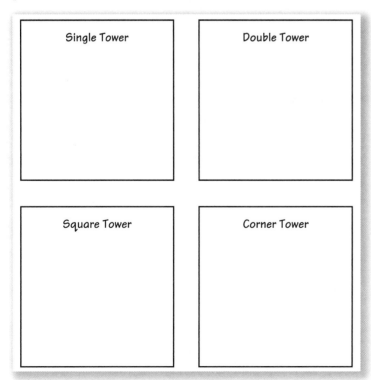

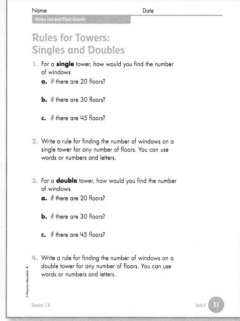

▲ Student Activity Book, p. 53

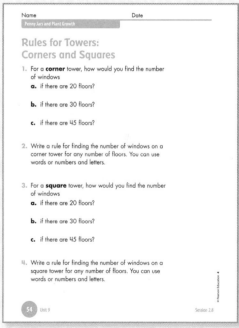

▲ Student Activity Book, p. 54

Although some students will write rules in symbolic form, such as $(6 \times n) + 2$, many will write rules in words, such as, "I multiplied the number of floors by 6 and then added 2." Both forms should be encouraged.

Students should complete rules for at least the single and double towers.

ONGOING ASSESSMENT: Observing Students at Work

Students work to create rules for each of the four types of towers.

- **Are students able to devise a rule for finding the number of windows in each type of tower for any number of floors?**

- **Can students relate the numbers in their rules to features of the tower?**

DIFFERENTIATION: Supporting the Range of Learners

Intervention If students are having difficulty formulating a rule, suggest that they add a third column to the tables on *Student Activity Book* pages 33–34 and 43–44 to write out the number of windows as addition or multiplication expressions. They can also refer to the *Student Math Handbook*.

Extension Students who complete their work can make graphs for each tower with the number of floors along the *x*-axis and the number of windows on the *y*-axis. Ask them to predict what the graph will look like before they draw it. They can compare the graphs of different towers in the way they compared Penny Jar graphs.

Also ask students who finish early whether they can apply the rule for a tower to a Penny Jar situation. If they wrote their rule in words, how can they change some of the words so that the situation is about a Penny Jar and not a tower? How are the floors and skylights similar to and different from the rounds and starting amount of a Penny Jar?

DISCUSSION

2 Rules for Towers

25 MIN   CLASS

Math Focus Points for Discussion

◆ Making rules that relate one variable to another in situations of constant change

◆ Using symbolic letter notation to represent the value of one variable in terms of another

Begin the discussion by looking at the various rules for the double tower. Are all of the different rules correct? Can each group defend its rule by showing how it relates to the features of the tower? Do all of the rules produce the same answers?❶

Can you use this rule to find any number of windows, no matter how many floors there are? What about 100 floors or 1,000 floors? How do you know?

In the course of this discussion, some of the rules may need to be revised. When the class has agreed on a set of rules for the double tower, ask questions to compare the different rules.

> multiply the number of floors by 6 and then add 2 to the number.
>
> First start with the 2 from the skylights and then add 6 windows for the sides for each floor the tower has.
>
> $(6 \times n) + 2$
>
> $2 + (F \times 6)$

Sample Student Work

Professional Development

❶ **Dialogue Box:** Rules for the Double Tower, p. 160

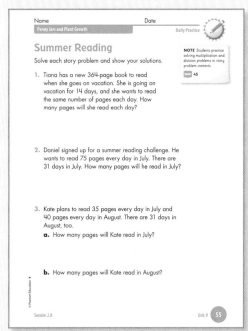

Name _____   Date _____

Penny Jars and Plant Growth   Daily Practice

Summer Reading

Solve each story problem and show your solutions.

NOTE Students practice solving multiplication and division problems in story problem contexts.

45

1. Tiana has a new 364-page book to read when she goes on vacation. She is going on vacation for 14 days, and she wants to read the same number of pages each day. How many pages will she read each day?

2. Daniel signed up for a summer reading challenge. He wants to read 75 pages every day in July. There are 31 days in July. How many pages will he read in July?

3. Kate plans to read 35 pages every day in July and 40 pages every day in August. There are 31 days in August, too.
   a. How many pages will Kate read in July?

   b. How many pages will Kate read in August?

Session 2.8   Unit 9   55

▲ **Student Activity Book, p. 55**

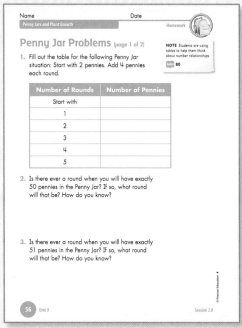

▲ Student Activity Book, p. 56

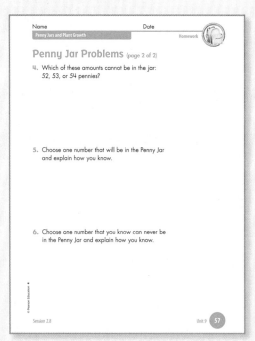

▲ Student Activity Book, p. 57

For rules written with symbols, different groups may have used different variable names (for example, n or F might both stand for "number of floors"). If so, the class will need to discuss why they can use either letter. For example $(6 \times n) + 2$ and $(6 \times F) + 2$ both define the same rule.

After you have listed rules for the double tower, pose a new question that brings back the Penny Jar situation.

One of your rules to find the number of windows for any number of floors in a double tower is $[(6 \times n) + 2]$. What if this rule applied to finding the total number of pennies in a Penny Jar situation? What could that Penny Jar situation be? What would the start number be for a Penny Jar situation with this rule? How many pennies would be added each day?

If time permits, discuss rules for either the corner or the square tower.

③ Daily Practice and Homework

 Daily Practice: For ongoing review, have students complete *Student Activity Book* page 55.

 Homework: On *Student Activity Book* pages 56–57, students fill in a table for a Penny Jar situation (Start with 2/Add 4 each round) and answer "backward problems" about whether certain amounts will ever be in the jar.

 Student Math Handbook: Students and families may use *Student Math Handbook* page 86 for reference and review. See pages 163–166 in the back of this unit.

Mathematical Emphases

Using Tables and Graphs Using graphs to represent change

Math Focus Points

◆ Identifying points in a graph with corresponding values in a table and interpreting the numerical information in terms of the situation the graph represents

◆ Plotting points on a coordinate grid to represent a situation in which one quantity is changing in relation to another

◆ Describing the relative steepness of graphs or parts of graphs in terms of different rates of change

◆ Comparing situations by describing the differences in their graphs

◆ Interpreting the points and shape of a graph in terms of the situation the graph represents

◆ Comparing tables, graphs, and situations of constant change with those of non-constant change

Using Tables and Graphs Using tables to represent change

Math Focus Points

◆ Using tables to represent the relationship between two quantities in a situation of constant change

Linear Change Describing and representing a constant rate of change

Math Focus Points

◆ Writing an arithmetic expression for finding the value of one quantity in terms of the other in a situation of constant change

This Investigation also focuses on

◆ Measuring in centimeters

Collecting and Analyzing Measurements

	Student Activity Book	Student Math Handbook	Professional Development: Read Ahead of Time	
SESSION 3.1 p. 106				
Graphing and Predicting Plant Growth Students make line graphs of plant growth. They examine how faster growth and slower growth are represented in a table and in a graph.	1–2, 59–62	72–77	• **Teacher Note:** Using Line Graphs to Represent Change, p. 133	
SESSION 3.2 p. 114				
Using Line Graphs to Compare Growth Students make a graph of two different plants on one set of axes. They compare the two graphs and write four or five statements about what they notice.	59–60, 63–64	75–77	• **Teacher Note:** Height or Change in Height?, p. 143	
SESSION 3.3 p. 119				
Graphs, Stories, and Tables Students match graphs with tables and stories. They discuss the connections between the description of change in a story and both the features of the graph and the values in the tables.	65–67	75–77		
SESSION 3.4 p. 124				
Straight or Not? Increasing or Decreasing? Students compare graphs of the different situations they have encountered in this unit. They create a table and a graph for a decreasing Penny Jar situation.	69–72	75–77	• **Dialogue Box:** Which Graphs Are Straight?, p. 162	
SESSION 3.5 p. 129				
End-of-Unit Assessment Students solve four problems that assess the benchmarks for this unit. In these problems, they compare graphs, write a story to match a graph, draw a graph to match a story, complete a table, and solve a problem about a situation of constant change.	73	75–77, 86	• **Teacher Note:** End-of-Unit Assessment, p. 145	

Materials to Gather	Materials to Prepare
• **Grid paper** (as needed) • **Colored pencils or markers** (as needed) • **T103, Fast and Slow Growth**	• **Blank transparencies or chart paper** On one sheet, create a two-column table with the headings *Day of the Week* and *Height*. Fill in the table with the following data set: Monday, 1.0 cm; Tuesday, 3.5 cm; Wednesday, 6.5 cm; Thursday, 7.5 cm; Friday, 9.0 cm. On a second sheet, create a blank graph with both axes drawn and even gridlines. Label the *x*-axis with the following 5 marks: *M, T, W, Th, F.* Leave room farther along the *x*-axis to add more days. Leave the *y*-axis unmarked.
• **Grid paper** (as needed) • **Colored pencils or markers** (as needed)	
• **Scissors** (1 pair) • **Glue or tape** • **Colored pencils or markers** (as needed)	• **M36, Matching Numbers, Stories, and Graphs** Make copies. (1 per pair)
	• **M37–M39, End-of-Unit Assessment** Make copies. (1 per student)

Overhead Transparency

Graphing and Predicting Plant Growth

Math Focus Points

◈ Identifying points in a graph with corresponding values in a table and interpreting the numerical information in terms of the situation the graph represents

◈ Plotting points on a coordinate grid to represent a situation in which one quantity is changing in relation to another

◈ Describing the relative steepness of graphs or parts of graphs in terms of different rates of change

Today's Plan		Materials
① **ACTIVITY** **Graphing Plant Heights**	30 MIN CLASS PAIRS	• *Student Activity Book,* pp. 1–2 (See Unit Preparation for Investigation 3) • Blank transparencies or chart paper*; grid paper; colored pencils or markers
② **DISCUSSION** **Fast and Slow Growth**	15 MIN CLASS	• *Student Activity Book,* p. 59 • T103
③ **ACTIVITY** **Graphing Fast and Slow Growth**	15 MIN PAIRS	• *Student Activity Book,* pp. 1–2 and 59–60 • Colored pencils or markers
④ **SESSION FOLLOW-UP** **Daily Practice and Homework**		• *Student Activity Book,* pp. 61–62 • *Student Math Handbook,* pp. 72–77

*See *Materials to Prepare,* p. 105.

Ten-Minute Math

Quick Survey For the survey, ask the class "How many times have you flown on an airplane?" or a different numerical question that you or the students choose. Make sure they collect data about something they already know or can observe easily. With today's data, make a line plot.

What do you notice about the data?

What do the data tell us about our class?

To prepare for the next Ten-Minute Math session, each student asks an adult at home how many times the adult has flown on an airplane.

ACTIVITY

30 MIN   CLASS   PAIRS

Graphing Plant Heights

Throughout this Investigation, unless otherwise specified, students who share a plant will work together. However, students should each produce their own graphs and complete the appropriate *Student Activity Book* pages.

In this activity, students make graphs of their plants' height. This is the first time that students will be setting up their own graphs on grid paper. Establish with the whole class how to label and mark the axes. Draw students' attention to the prepared table and the graph that you have begun.

Day of the Week	Height
Monday	1.0 cm
Tuesday	3.5 cm
Wednesday	6.5 cm
Thursday	7.5 cm
Friday	9.0 cm

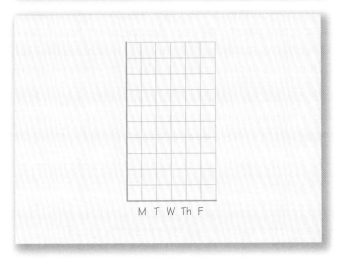

M T W Th F

This graph is going to show how tall your plant was on each day. I want you to think about how I should mark the vertical axis. What will "high up" mean on this graph? What will "low down" mean?

Professional Development

❶ Teacher Note: Using Line Graphs to Represent Change, p. 133

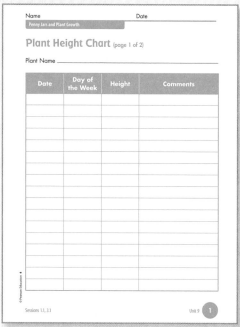

▲ **Student Activity Book, p. 1**

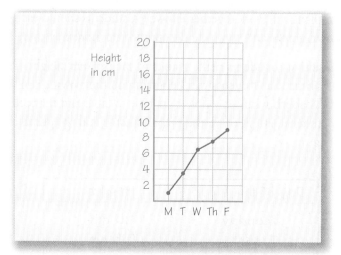

Ask students for ideas about how to mark the *y*-axis. After settling any disagreements, mark the *y*-axis in regular intervals. Then plot the five heights listed in the table, reviewing with students how to plot and interpret points as needed.

Although students have had experience both interpreting and creating graphs throughout this unit, making their own graphs on graph paper can be challenging.❶ Remind them of the graphs of temperature that they made in Investigation 1, which they can use as visual references.

Students use the information on *Student Activity Book* pages 1–2 to make graphs, on graph paper, that show the heights of their plants over the first 5 days of measurement. If students have missing data, ask them to think about what to do for days on which they have no measurements.

As students work, ask questions that connect the height of the plants with the information shown in the graph. In addition, ask questions drawing attention to how the graph shows changes in the plant growth.

- What does this point mean? Where in the table is this point on the graph?

- Did your plant grow steadily, fast, or slowly between these two days? How can you tell that from the graph?

After students have plotted points for the first 5 days, call the class together for a few minutes to pose a new question.

Now that you have entered information on the graph for the first 5 days, set your Plant Height Chart aside and look at the graph. Predict how you think the graph will continue. How do you think your graph will look after you have plotted points for another week?

▲ **Student Activity Book, p. 2**

Students should mark their predictions on their graphs in a different color or with dotted lines and then write out an explanation for their predictions. Some students may think that their plants will continue to grow in the same way; others may think that their plants will speed up or slow down. The accuracy of their predictions is not important. What is important is that students are representing their predictions on their graphs.

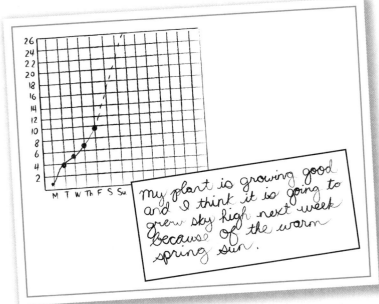

Sample Student Work

ONGOING ASSESSMENT: Observing Students at Work

Students graph the first 5 days of plant growth, and then they extend the graph to show predicted growth. Students create a story that supports the prediction.

- **Do students mark the vertical axis with a consistent scale?**

- **If data is missing, do students skip over that day on the horizontal axis?**

- **Do students represent the data from their table correctly on the graph?**

- **Does the predicted graph shape match the written explanation?**
  For example, if students say the plant will continue to grow fast, is the growth represented on the graph accurately?

Math Note

❷ **Growth Over Time** In order to compare the Friday–Monday period to the Monday–Tuesday period, students need to understand that the greater amount of growth (6 centimeters) took place over three days, whereas the 3.5-centimeter growth took place over only one day. Even though 6 centimeters is a larger amount of growth, that growth was spread over a longer period of time. Some students might think of the 6-centimeter growth as an average of 2 centimeters per day spread over three days, in comparison to the 3.5 centimeters in the one-day period from Monday's measurement to Tuesday's measurement. The graph is steeper in the Monday to Tuesday period, indicating faster growth.

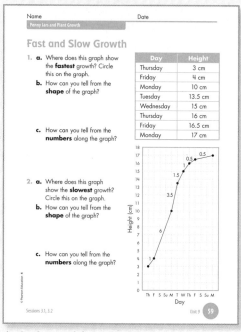

▲ Student Activity Book, p. 59;
Transparencies, T103

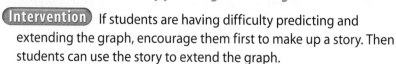

DIFFERENTIATION: Supporting the Range of Learners

Intervention If students are having difficulty predicting and extending the graph, encourage them first to make up a story. Then students can use the story to extend the graph.

In your story, does your plant grow slowly? Quickly? How would that look on the graph?

Remind students of the temperature graphs from the beginning of this unit. What did the graph look like when the temperature increased slowly? What did the graph look like when the temperature increased quickly?

ELL For this work with graphs of plant height, make sure that students know the English names for the days of the week. Have students circle the letter or letters in each name that correspond with the abbreviations appearing on the x-axis.

DISCUSSION

❷ **Fast and Slow Growth**

15 MIN   CLASS

Math Focus Points for Discussion

◆ Identifying points in a graph with corresponding values in a table and interpreting the numerical information in terms of the situation the graph represents

◆ Describing the relative steepness of graphs or parts of graphs in terms of different rates of change

Students turn to *Student Activity Book* page 59. Note that the horizontal axis shows every day of the week. There are no dots on the graph indicating height values for the weekend days, however.

Allow 5 minutes for students to talk in pairs and write answers to the questions on the *Student Activity Book* page. Then display the transparency Fast and Slow Growth (T103).

Focus this discussion on the questions next to the graph.

• Where does this graph show the fastest growth? How can you tell from the shape of the graph? How can you tell from the numbers along the graph's axes?

• Some people think that the plant grew fastest on the weekend. Other people think that it grew fastest from Monday to Tuesday. What do you think? ❷

Students describe how the graph shows changes in the rate of plant growth.

Students might say:

"It's really steep from Monday to Tuesday, so that was the fastest growth."

"You can tell by the numbers. Most of the days it's only around 1 centimeter, but from Monday to Tuesday it's 3.5."

"It grew more than that on the weekend. It grew 6 centimeters."

"But that was more than just one day. It was like 3 days. If it grew 3.5 from Friday to Saturday and then another 3.5 from Saturday to Sunday and then another 3.5 from Sunday to Monday, that would be a lot more than 6."

Students might want to think about what the actual measurement could have been for those three days to total 6 centimeters. Breaking the total measurement into individual measurements for each day can help them compare the rate of growth on the weekend to the rate of growth between the Monday and Tuesday measurements.❸

Ask similar questions about the slowest growth.

Math Note

❸ **Average Rate of Growth** Because measurements were not taken on the weekend, the line between Friday's and Monday's measurements represents an average rate of growth during that period. During that period, however, the rate of growth could have varied. For example, suppose that the plant grew 1 centimeter from Friday to Saturday; 1.5 centimeters from Saturday to Sunday; and 3.5 centimeters from Sunday to Monday. In that case, the rate of growth from Sunday to Monday would be the same as from Monday to Tuesday. Alternatively, if the plant grew 2 centimeters during each of the three weekend periods, the rate throughout the entire weekend was slower than the rate from Monday to Tuesday. Students might bring up these ideas, or they might focus on comparing the average rates by looking at the slope of the line on the graph. Both of these approaches are reasonable.

Name _____ **Date** _____

Penny Jars and Plant Growth

Our Growing Plants

Use this sheet with the graph you have made of your growing plant.

1. On the graph of your growing plant, write the changes (in centimeters) on each section of the line.

2. Find a place on your graph where your plant was growing quickly. Write the word "fast" along your graph in this place.

3. Explain how you know this is fast growth. Look at the shape of the graph and at the numbers on your graph.

4. Find a place on your graph where your plant was growing more slowly. Write the word "slow" along your graph in this place.

5. Explain how you know this is slow growth. Look at the shape of the graph and at the numbers on your graph.

60   Unit 9   Sessions 3.1, 3.2

© Pearson Education 4

▲ **Student Activity Book, p. 60** PORTFOLIO

ACTIVITY

3 Graphing Fast and Slow Growth

15 MIN   PAIRS

In this activity, students continue working on their own graphs. Using their original pencil color, they add to their graphs as many actual measurements as they have recorded on *Student Activity Book* pages 1–2. If they have enough data, they should compare the predictions that they made earlier with their plants' actual growth.

Students use *Student Activity Book* page 60 to record the changes in their plants' heights. *Student Activity Book* page 59 can provide a model for how to label the changes in height along the graph.

Students work in pairs to finish graphing and describing the growth of their plants.

As students are working, check their explanations to see whether they understand how both the shape of the graph and the numbers in the table reflect the speed of their plants' growth.

ONGOING ASSESSMENT: Observing Students at Work

Students use their graphs to answer questions about how the graph shows faster and slower growth.

- **Do students associate periods of fast growth with the steepest part of the graph?**

- **Do students associate periods of slow growth with the less steep part of the graph?**

- **Do students graph missing measurements appropriately?**

DIFFERENTIATION: Supporting the Range of Learners

Intervention Suggest that students who are having difficulty interpreting the meaning of "faster" or "slower" growth add a third column to the table on *Student Activity Book* pages 1–2. In this column, they can record the amount of change from day to day (for example, from Monday to Tuesday, it grew 2 cm). Then talk with students about which days the plant growth was greatest and what that looks like on their graphs. Students can also look at the graphs of different rates of growth in the *Student Math Handbook*.

SESSION FOLLOW-UP

4 Daily Practice and Homework

 Daily Practice: For reinforcement of this unit's content, have students complete *Student Activity Book* page 61.

 Homework: For a review of multiplication, have students complete *Student Activity Book* page 62.

 Student Math Handbook: Students and families may use *Student Math Handbook* pages 72–77 for reference and review. See pages 163–166 in the back of this unit.

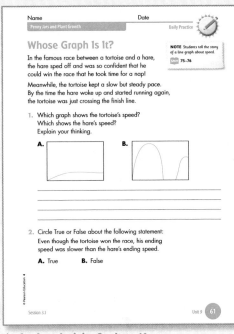

▲ Student Activity Book, p. 61

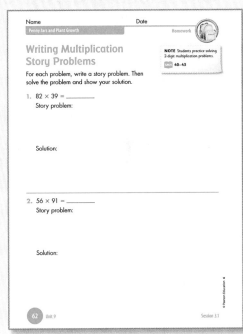

▲ Student Activity Book, p. 62

Using Line Graphs to Compare Growth

Math Focus Points

◆ Plotting points on a coordinate grid to represent a situation in which one quantity is changing in relation to another

◆ Comparing situations by describing the differences in their graphs

◆ Describing the relative steepness of graphs or parts of graphs in terms of different rates of change

Today's Plan		Materials
1 ACTIVITY **Comparing Growth of Different Plants**	40 MIN PAIRS GROUPS	• *Student Activity Book,* pp. 59–60 (from Session 3.1) • Students' completed graphs of plant growth from Session 3.1; grid paper; colored pencils or markers
2 DISCUSSION **Comparing Plants**	20 MIN CLASS	• Completed graphs (From Activity 1)
3 SESSION FOLLOW-UP **Daily Practice and Homework**		• *Student Activity Book,* pp. 63–64 • *Student Math Handbook,* pp. 75–77

Ten-Minute Math

Quick Survey For the survey, collect data about adults' responses to "How many times have you flown on an airplane?" Add today's data to the line plot created in the previous session and ask students to make comparisons.

• What do you notice about our data today?

• How are today's data the same as last session's?

• How are they different?

• What does that tell us about our class?

ACTIVITY

① Comparing Growth of Different Plants

40 MIN   PAIRS   GROUPS

In this activity, students work in groups of four: two pairs of students, each pair working with their own plant. Each student from the first pair teams with one of the students from the second pair. In these new pairs, students graph the growth of both plants (as recorded on their graphs from Session 3.1) on the same set of axes. When both of the new pairs have completed their graphs, the pairs work together as a group of four to compare the graphs and to write statements that describe and compare the graphs.

Today you will compare the ways two of your plants have been growing by putting the growth of both plants on the same piece of grid paper, using the same set of axes—just as we did with the Penny Jar Comparisons. You will need to decide together how to set up your graph and what to put along each axis of the new graph. Once you have decided this, graph both plants using a different color for each plant.

Both members of a pair work on the same sheet of paper, so each pair makes only one set of graphs. As pairs finish, students rejoin their original partners, making groups of four. First, they compare the ways they graphed the two plants and the ways the plants grew. As they work, ask questions inviting students to compare the graphs:

What numbers did you put along the axis for the heights of the plants? How did you decide what numbers to use? What is similar about the growth of the two plants? What is different about their growth?

Using a space on the grid paper or a new sheet of paper, each group writes four or five statements about their graphs, comparing the ways their plants grew. These statements are the basis for the whole-group discussion at the end of the session.

Groups compare the growth of two plants and note their observations.

ONGOING ASSESSMENT: Observing Students at Work

Students work with a new partner to make a graph that shows each of their plants' growth, and then re-join their original partners to compare and make statements about the graphs.

- **Do students look at both sets of data to determine a scale for the vertical axis?**

- **Do students make statements comparing the heights of the two plants?**

- **Do students make statements comparing the change in the heights of the plants (for example, fast growth compared to slow growth)?**

DIFFERENTIATION: Supporting the Range of Learners

(**Intervention**) Students who have difficulty starting the graph can use the graph from *Student Activity Book* page 59, as well as their completed graphs from the previous session, as models for making their own. Students can also use their completed *Student Activity Book* page 60 to get started on making statements comparing the two graphs.

Professional Development

❶ **Teacher Note:** Height or Change in Height?, p. 143

DISCUSSION

② Comparing Plants

20 MIN   CLASS

Math Focus Points for Discussion

◆ Comparing situations by describing differences in their graphs

◆ Describing the relative steepness of graphs or parts of graphs in terms of different rates of change

In this discussion, provide time for each group to show their graphs and to read their statements. For each statement, ask questions linking the plant growth situation to the graph. For instance, if students say, "Both plants went up steadily," ask questions such as:

How do you see that on the graph? What part of the graph are you looking at?❶

If there is time, ask students what they saw on the combined graphs that was different from what they saw on the individual graphs.

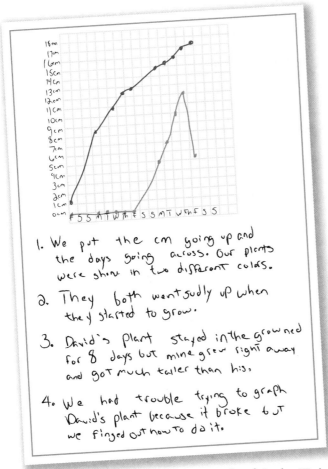

Sample Student Work

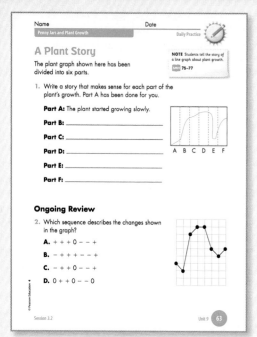

A Plant Story

The plant graph shown here has been divided into six parts.

NOTE Students tell the story of a line graph about plant growth. SMH 75–77

1. Write a story that makes sense for each part of the plant's growth. Part A has been done for you.

Part A: The plant started growing slowly.

Part B: _____

Part C: _____

Part D: _____

Part E: _____

Part F: _____

Ongoing Review

2. Which sequence describes the changes shown in the graph?

A. + + + 0 − − +
B. − + + + − − +
C. − + + 0 − − +
D. 0 + + 0 − − 0

Session 3.2 Unit 9 63

▲ Student Activity Book, p. 63

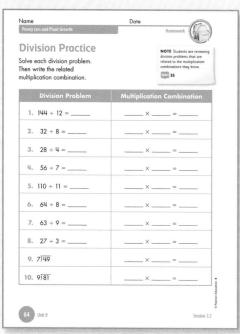

Division Practice

Solve each division problem. Then write the related multiplication combination.

NOTE Students are reviewing division problems that are related to the multiplication combinations they know. SMH 35

Division Problem	Multiplication Combination
1. 144 ÷ 12 = _____	____ × ____ = ____
2. 32 ÷ 8 = _____	____ × ____ = ____
3. 28 ÷ 4 = _____	____ × ____ = ____
4. 56 ÷ 7 = _____	____ × ____ = ____
5. 110 ÷ 11 = _____	____ × ____ = ____
6. 64 ÷ 8 = _____	____ × ____ = ____
7. 63 ÷ 9 = _____	____ × ____ = ____
8. 27 ÷ 3 = _____	____ × ____ = ____
9. 7)49	____ × ____ = ____
10. 9)81	____ × ____ = ____

64 Unit 9 Session 3.2

▲ Student Activity Book, p. 64

At the end of the discussion, ask students to consider all of the plants in the class. Overall, have most of the plants grown in a similar way, or are some different from the others? What would students expect if they planted more beans? Is there a usual pattern of growth?

SESSION FOLLOW-UP

③ Daily Practice and Homework

 Daily Practice: For reinforcement of this unit's content, have students complete *Student Activity Book* page 63.

 Homework: For a review of division, have students complete *Student Activity Book* page 64.

Student Math Handbook: Students and families may use *Student Math Handbook* pages 75–77 for reference and review. See pages 163–166 in the back of this unit.

Graphs, Stories, and Tables

Math Focus Points

◆ Identifying points in a graph with corresponding values in a table and interpreting the numerical information in terms of the situation the graph represents

Today's Plan		Materials
ACTIVITY **①** **Matching Numbers, Stories, and Graphs**	45 MIN CLASS PAIRS	• M36* • Scissors; glue or tape; colored pencils or markers
DISCUSSION **②** **What Does the Graph Show?**	15 MIN CLASS	• M36
SESSION FOLLOW-UP **③** **Daily Practice and Homework**		• *Student Activity Book,* pp. 65–67 • *Student Math Handbook,* pp. 75–77

*See *Materials to Prepare,* p. 105.

Ten-Minute Math

Closest Estimate Show Problems 19, 20, and 21 on *Closest Estimate* (T93) one at a time. Give students approximately 30 seconds to look at the three possible estimates that are provided and determine which is the closest to the actual answer. Have two or three students explain their reasoning for each problem.

How did you break the numbers apart?

How did you determine the magnitude of your answer?

If you changed the numbers in the problem, how did you change them and why?

Is the closest estimate greater than or less than the actual answer?

How do you know?

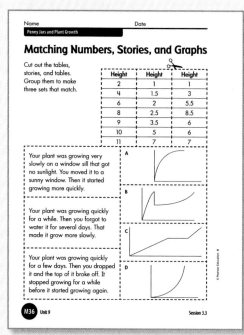

▲ **Transparencies, T93**

▲ **Resource Masters, M36**

45 MIN   CLASS   PAIRS

ACTIVITY

Matching Numbers, Stories, and Graphs

Introduce this activity by discussing an example of the way the shape of a graph tells a story about how a plant grew. Sketch the following graph (without putting any values on the axes), and ask students what it indicates about the plant.

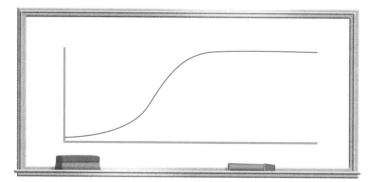

Here is a graph that shows how a plant grew. How would you describe the plant's growth?

Students may say that at first, the plant grew slowly; then it started to grow more quickly; then it slowed down and stopped growing. Invite students to point out the sections of the graph that match each description.

Let's talk about some measurements that could result in this graph. What might the first measurement be? Where would that be on the graph? What could the next measurement be? Where would that be on the graph?

List their suggestions on the board. A reasonable sequence of numbers, for example, might be 2 cm, 3 cm, 4 cm, 7 cm, 10 cm, 11 cm, 11 cm. Ask students how the sequence of numbers matches the graph and their descriptions.

Students now work on Matching Numbers, Stories, and Graphs (M36), to show the way a story, a table, and a graph can represent the same situation. Note that there are three complete situations on this student sheet; the sheet also includes one graph that does not correspond with any of the tables or stories. First, students cut out the graphs, the tables of plant heights, and the stories. Then, they group together those that correspond and affix each set to a sheet of paper. Once they have three complete sets, they write a story and make a list of heights that could correspond to the fourth graph.

As you circulate, ask questions to focus attention on connecting features of the graph with the story and the table of heights.

- Where is the largest change in the measurement list? What is happening to the plant at that time? Where is the fastest growth shown on the graph?

- Where is the plant growing the least? How do you see that in the table? How do you see that in the graph?

As you observe the students making their own stories and heights to match the fourth graph, choose two or three students to present their work during the whole-class discussion.

As students finish, make small groups to discuss how they matched the graphs, stories, and tables. If there is disagreement in a group, encourage students to explain their ideas to one another.

ONGOING ASSESSMENT: Observing Students at Work

Students cut out the tables, graphs, and stories and glue each matching series on a separate sheet of paper. They make up their own story and table of values for the remaining graph.

- **Do students associate smaller changes over a certain period of time (as shown in the table) with slower growth and larger changes over the same amount of time with faster growth?**

- **Do students associate slower growth with less steep sections of the graph and faster growth with steeper sections?**

- **Can students develop a plant-growth story and a list of height measurements that matches Graph C?**

DIFFERENTIATION: Supporting the Range of Learners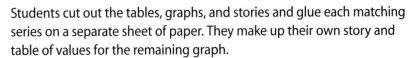

Intervention Suggest that students having difficulty choosing the table of heights that goes with a particular graph and story first make their own graphs for each list of measurements. Or, work with a small group of students to mark each section of the graphs with phrases such as "grew more slowly" and "grew faster," as students did in previous sessions. Then they can look at the stories to see which stories match what they wrote on the graphs.

ELL Read each story aloud and ask students to paraphrase it. Have them underline key words and phrases: *very slowly, more quickly, started, stopped.* Make sure they understand that one of the graphs does not represent any of the given stories.

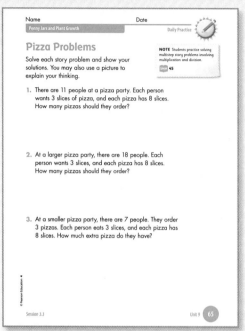

▲ Student Activity Book, p. 65

Name _____ Date _____
Penny Jars and Plant Growth | Daily Practice

Pizza Problems

Solve each story problem and show your solutions. You may also use a picture to explain your thinking.

NOTE Students practice solving multistep story problems involving multiplication and division.

1. There are 11 people at a pizza party. Each person wants 3 slices of pizza, and each pizza has 8 slices. How many pizzas should they order?

2. At a larger pizza party, there are 18 people. Each person wants 3 slices, and each pizza has 8 slices. How many pizzas should they order?

3. At a smaller pizza party, there are 7 people. They order 3 pizzas. Each person eats 3 slices, and each pizza has 8 slices. How much extra pizza do they have?

Session 3.3 | Unit 9 65

15 MIN   CLASS

DISCUSSION
What Does the Graph Show?

Math Focus Points for Discussion

◈ Identifying points in a graph with corresponding values in a table and interpreting the numerical information in terms of the situation the graph represents

Begin by having students explain how they determined which graph went with each story and each table. Continue asking questions that focus on the way fast and slow change appears in each representation.

Turn to the fourth graph and solicit two or three stories. As students tell their stories, have them point to the parts of the graph that correspond to their descriptions. Ask the rest of the class to comment on the stories and to bring up any questions or different ways of thinking about the graph.

Students might say:

"It was growing kind of steadily for a while, and then it stopped and just stayed the same height for a day or two. Then I moved it to a spot where it got more sun, and it shot up really fast."

"It was growing fast. Then I forgot to water it for a couple of days, and it stopped growing. Then I added some fertilizer, and it started growing even faster than before."

On the board, list one or two sets of plant heights that students created to match the graph. Ask students to describe why these lists of heights make sense.

Here is the list of heights that Marisol suggested. How does this list match her story? Which height measurements go with the part of her story in which she forgot to water the plant? Which measurements go with the part in which the plant was growing even faster than before? How can you tell from the graph that the plant is growing faster than it was at the beginning?

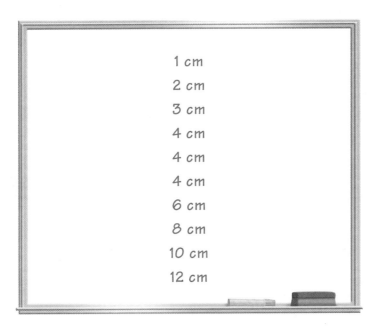

1 cm

2 cm

3 cm

4 cm

4 cm

4 cm

6 cm

8 cm

10 cm

12 cm

SESSION FOLLOW-UP

③ Daily Practice and Homework

 Daily Practice: For ongoing review, have students complete *Student Activity Book* page 65.

 Homework: Students work on a Penny Jar situation on *Student Activity Book* pages 66–67. Part of the purpose of this homework is to review the Penny Jar situations since some of tomorrow's class focuses on comparing all of the situations they have encountered in this unit.

Student Math Handbook: Students and families may use *Student Math Handbook* pages 75–77 for reference and review. See pages 162–165 in the back of this unit.

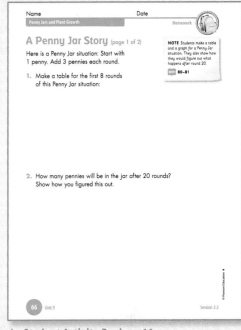

▲ **Student Activity Book, p. 66**

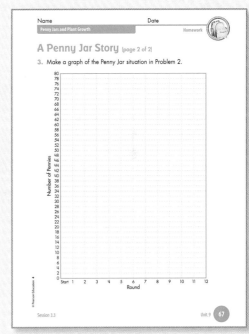

▲ **Student Activity Book, p. 67**

Straight or Not? Increasing or Decreasing?

Math Focus Points

- Interpreting the points and shape of a graph in terms of the situation the graph represents
- Comparing tables, graphs, and situations of constant change with those of non-constant change
- Plotting points on a coordinate grid to represent a situation in which one quantity is changing in relation to another

Vocabulary

decrease

Today's Plan		Materials
1 DISCUSSION **Comparing Graphs**	25 MIN CLASS	• Students' completed work, particularly graphs, from throughout this Investigation
2 ACTIVITY **Removing Pennies from a Penny Jar**	35 MIN CLASS PAIRS	• Student Activity Book, pp. 69–70
3 SESSION FOLLOW-UP **Daily Practice and Homework**		• Student Activity Book, pp. 71–72 • Student Math Handbook, pp. 75–76, 77

Ten-Minute Math

Closest Estimate Show Problems 22, 23, and 24 on *Closest Estimate* (T93) one at a time. Give students approximately 30 seconds to look at the three possible estimates that are provided and to determine which is the closest to the actual answer. Have two or three students explain their reasoning for each problem.

How did you break the numbers apart?

How did you determine the magnitude of your answer?

If you changed the numbers in the problem, how did you change them, and why?

Is the closest estimate greater than or less than the actual answer?

How do you know?

DISCUSSION

Comparing Graphs

25 MIN   CLASS

Math Focus Points for Discussion

◆ Comparing tables, graphs, and situations of constant change with situations of non-constant change

In this discussion, students compare the graphs of the different situations they have encountered in this unit—temperature, speed, Penny Jars, Windows and Towers, and plant growth. ❶ It is helpful if students have available their work on the different kinds of graphs. They can refer to this work during the discussion.

We are finishing up our unit on describing and representing situations in which something is growing or changing over time. Think about the different kinds of situations that we graphed during this unit. As you name them, I'll list them.

> Speed
> Temperature
> Penny Jars
> Windows and Towers
> Plant growth

You can also ask students whether they know of any other kinds of graphs that show something growing or changing over time.

Think about the shapes of the graphs for these different situations. Are there ways in which the graph or some parts of the graph for each of these is the same as for other situations? How are they the same? How are they different?

Ask students to justify their statements by referring to specific graphs or parts of graphs. Encourage students to point to examples in the room, to show examples from their previous work, and to use their hands to indicate the shape of a graph. Students might notice that:

• Graphs for the Penny Jar and Windows and Towers are straight, showing a constant rate of change.

- Graphs for speed, temperature, and plant growth are not straight. Their rate of change varies.

- Graphs of the Penny Jar and Windows and Towers only increase, while the other graphs both increase and decrease over time. (Plant height is generally expected to increase, except in the instance of the plant breaking off, as in one of our examples.)

- The Penny Jar and Windows and Towers are artificial situations designed so that there is a steady increase. The stories could be changed to situations that do not have a constant rate of change. The speed, temperature, and plant-growth situations, on the other hand, are real data. They are affected by many things that happen in the real world. For example, the plants might be affected by the amount of sun or water they get or by whether they have been fertilized.

Depending on what students bring up, follow-up questions can include

- Which of these graphs are straight lines? Which are not? Why is that?

- Could a graph for temperature, speed, or plant growth be straight? What would that mean if it were straight? Why do you think that could happen, or why not? Did it happen for any of our plants?

- Could a Penny Jar or Windows and Towers situation decrease instead of increase? What would the story be for a Penny Jar that decreased?

Students may notice that part of a graph showing temperature or plant growth might be straight, showing a constant rate of growth for a short period of time, but that it is unlikely that over a long period of time, a plant or the temperature would behave like a Penny Jar.

35 MIN   CLASS   PAIRS

ACTIVITY

Removing Pennies from a Penny Jar

Introduce this activity by referring to the previous discussion; or, if it did not come up, introduce the idea yourself.

You noticed that our Penny Jar situations only increased, but Barney said that we could have a Penny Jar that decreased. For our last activity in this unit, we're going to experiment with what that would look like. Can anyone think of a story for a Penny Jar that would give us a constant rate of change with the change decreasing?

Emphasize that when you were increasing the number of pennies, you added the same number each day. Explain that you now want a situation in which the number of pennies decreases by the same amount each day.

Who can show us with your hand what a graph of a decreasing Penny Jar situation would look like? Why do you think it would look like that?

Spend no more than 10 minutes on this introduction because students will need time to work on the activity. At the end of the session, you can return to a brief discussion of what students noticed.

Students now work on *Student Activity Book* pages 69–70.

Students make a graph that shows the number of pennies in the Penny Jar decreasing.

As students are working, circulate and ask them questions that connect the situation, the table, and the graph:

• What do you notice in this graph?

• Why is the graph shaped this way?

• How does what you see in the graph connect to the numbers in the table? Could you tell from the table what the graph would look like?

• How is the table the same as, and how is it different from, the other Penny Jar situations we worked on? How is the graph the same as, and how is it different from, the graphs of other Penny Jar situations?

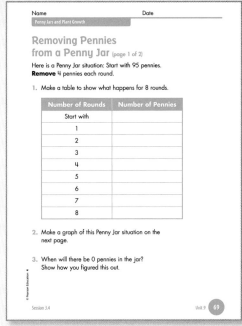

▲ Student Activity Book, p. 69

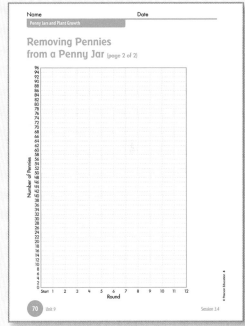

▲ Student Activity Book, p. 70

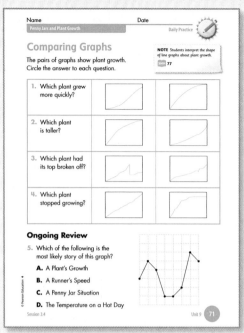

▲ Student Activity Book, p. 71

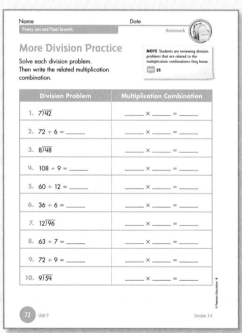

▲ Student Activity Book, p. 72

If you have time at the end of the session, use these same questions in a brief whole-class discussion, or ask students how they figured out at what point there will be no pennies in the jar.

ONGOING ASSESSMENT: Observing Students at Work

Students make a table and a graph for a Penny Jar situation in which pennies are removed from the jar at a constant rate.

- **Do students notice that the constant decreasing rate is shown by the sequence of values in the table?**

- **Do students understand how the shape of the graph matches the situation?**

DIFFERENTIATION: Supporting the Range of Learners

Intervention Some students may have difficulty getting started because they are so familiar with Penny Jar situations that begin with a small number of pennies and then increase. Ask whether there are some students who would like to get started with you. Work with that small group to fill in the first few rows of the table and to plot the first few points on the graph.

Extension Students who easily complete the table and graph can work on developing a rule for predicting the number of pennies in a jar for any round.

SESSION FOLLOW-UP
③ Daily Practice and Homework

 Daily Practice: For reinforcement of this unit's content, have students complete *Student Activity Book* page 71.

 Homework: For a review of division, have students complete *Student Activity Book* page 72.

 Student Math Handbook: Students and families may use *Student Math Handbook* pages 75–76, 77 for reference and review. See pages 163–166 in the back of this unit.

End-of-Unit Assessment

Math Focus Points

◆ Describing the relative steepness of graphs or parts of graphs in terms of different rates of change

◆ Using tables to represent the relationship between two quantities in a situation of constant change

◆ Writing an arithmetic expression for finding the value of one quantity in terms of the other in a situation of constant change

Today's Plan		Materials
① ASSESSMENT ACTIVITY **End-of-Unit Assessment**	✔ 🕐 👤 60 MIN INDIVIDUALS	• M37–M39*
② SESSION FOLLOW-UP **Daily Practice**		• *Student Activity Book*, p. 73 • *Student Math Handbook*, pp. 75–77, 86

*See *Materials to Prepare*, p. 105.

Ten-Minute Math

Quick Survey For the survey ask the class to choose a question that will result in numerical data (i.e., a question for which each person responds with a quantity, such as "How many cousins do you have?"). With today's data, make a line plot. Ask:

• What do you notice about the data?

• What do the data tell us about our class?

1 **Teacher Note:** End-of-Unit Assessment, p. 145

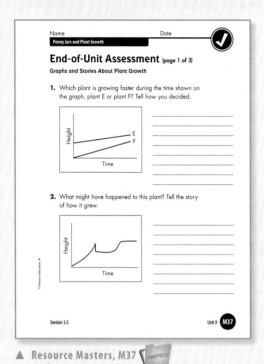

▲ **Resource Masters, M37** [PORTFOLIO]

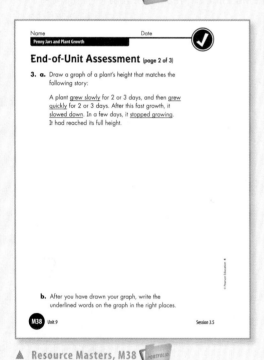

▲ **Resource Masters, M38** [PORTFOLIO]

ASSESSMENT ACTIVITY

① End-of-Unit Assessment

60 MIN **INDIVIDUALS**

The End-of-Unit Assessment (M37–M39) assesses students on four of the benchmarks for this unit. **①**

Problems 1–3 focus on plant growth. Students first compare two lines on a graph to decide which plant is growing faster. They write a plant-growth story to match another line graph, and they sketch and label a graph to match a given story. These problems address Benchmark 1: Connect tables and graphs to each other and to the situations they represent, and Benchmark 3: Describe how a graph shows change: where the rate of change is increasing, decreasing, or remaining constant, and how differences in steepness represent differences in the rate of change.

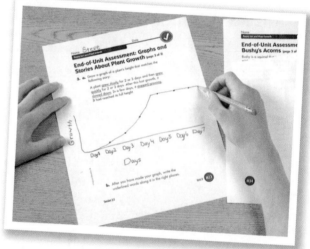

Students create a graph to accompany a story about plant growth.

Problems 4 and 5 refer to a situation of constant change: A squirrel has 5 acorns, then collects 3 acorns each day. Students complete a table for days 1–7, 10, 15, and 20. Then they write an arithmetic expression to show how many acorns the squirrel will have after 100 days. These problems again address Benchmark 1, as well as Benchmark 4: Take into account the starting amount and the amount of change in describing and comparing situations of constant change, and Benchmark 5: In a situation of constant change, write rules (using words or arithmetic expressions) to determine the value of one quantity, given the value of the other.

In Problem 4, remind students to pay attention to the fact that the table skips some rounds. Although students should by now expect that tables can skip values, it is important for the assessment that students are clear that they should find the number of acorns for days 10, 15, and 20.

Students who finish before the end of the session may return to activities from previous sessions.

If you have time at the end of this session or later in the day, ask students to share their ideas about each of these problems.

ONGOING ASSESSMENT: Observing Students at Work

Students interpret graphs of plant growth and match graphs and stories (Problems 1–3). They also complete a table and write an arithmetic expression for a situation of constant change (Problems 4–5).

- **How do students interpret graphs of change over time?** Do they determine which of two graphs represent faster or slower change? Do they describe parts of a graph as representing increasing change or no change?

- **How do students represent change over time on a graph?** Do they use relative steepness of parts of a graph to represent slower or faster change?

- **Can students correctly match the parts of a story about growth to those parts of a graph that represent that story?**

- **Can students correctly complete a table that represents a situation of constant change?**

- **Can students write an arithmetic expression that correctly takes into account the starting amount and the constant change?**

SESSION FOLLOW-UP
2 Daily Practice

Daily Practice: For enrichment, have students complete *Student Activity Book* page 73. This page provides real-world problems involving the math content of this unit.

Student Math Handbook: Students and families may use *Student Math Handbook* pages 75–77, 86 for reference and review. See pages 162–165 in the back of this unit.

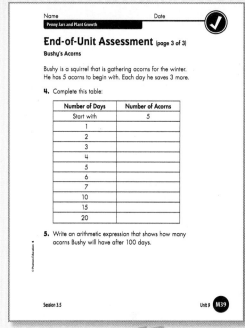

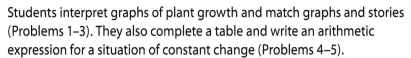

▲ Resource Masters, M39

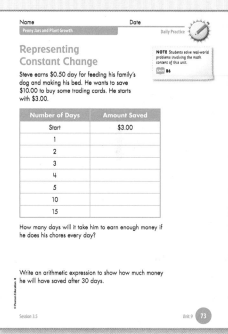

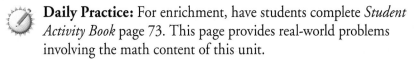

▲ Student Activity Book, p. 73

Penny Jars and Plant Growth

In Part 6 of *Implementing Investigations in Grade 4,* you will find a set of Teacher Notes that addresses topics and issues applicable to the curriculum as a whole rather than to specific curriculum units. They include the following:

Computational Fluency and Place Value

Computational Algorithms and Methods

Representations and Contexts for Mathematical Work

Foundations of Algebra in the Elementary Grades

Discussing Mathematical Ideas

Racial and Linguistic Diversity in the Classroom:
    What Does Equity Mean in Today's Math Classroom?

Teacher Note

Using Line Graphs to Represent Change

In Investigations 1 and 3, students use and interpret graphs that show how one quantity, such as speed, temperature, or the height of a plant, changes over time. In Investigation 2, students consider the relationship between other kinds of quantities, such as the number of windows on a tower and the number of floors of the tower. From their work on temperature in Grade 3, students may be familiar with line graphs to show the relationship between two quantities. However, keep in mind that when students learn to use a conventional representation such as a line graph, aspects of the meaning of the representation that adults take for granted may not be obvious to students who have less experience with it.

Many students will be more experienced with graphs that show the *frequency* of something. These graphs—such as line plots or bar graphs—show the *frequency* with which different values of one quantity occur. For example, this line plot shows the number of cavities in a group of children who visited a dentist during a particular week. It shows how many times each value (2 cavities, 3 cavities, etc.) occurs:

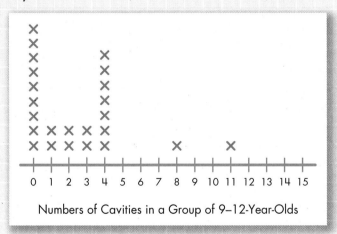

Numbers of Cavities in a Group of 9–12-Year-Olds

In this unit, students encounter a very different kind of graph. Line graphs show a *relationship between two quantities* (i.e., temperature and time or plant height and time). When students first encounter these new kinds of situations in which they must relate change in one quantity to change in another, they may try to use what they know about bar graphs and line plots to represent changing quantities. For example, here is a representation that one student created in Investigation 2, Session 2.1, to show how the number of pennies in a jar varies with the number of rounds:

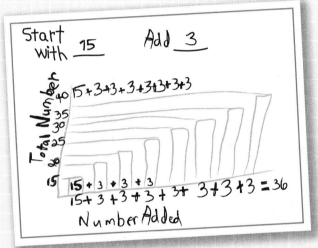

Sample Student Work

Conventions of Line Graphs

As students review the use of line graphs to represent temperature and motion in Investigation 1, help them work with the conventions of this kind of graphing. Students who do not have experience with line graphs may not understand that a point on the graph represents *two* values and is plotted at the *intersection* of a vertical line from the value of the quantity on the *x*-axis and a horizontal line from the value of the quantity on the *y*-axis. In the line graph on the next page, in order to read the temperature in Moscow on April 8, you must find where the vertical line that starts at April 8 on the horizontal axis intersects the temperature lines, and then move horizontally to the *y*-axis to read the temperature value of 50 degrees. Even if there are not actual lines on the page, you can imagine the intersection of such lines in order to read the information on the graph. For example, to read the temperature in Moscow on February 25, imagine a horizontal line from about 22 degrees intersecting the temperature lines at that point. It may seem natural that a point can represent two values (for example, a temperature of 50 degrees and a point in time such as April 8), but students must gain experience in learning to read this conventional representation.

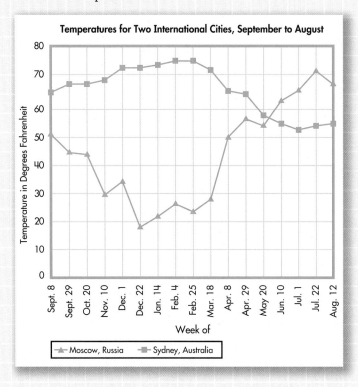

Another convention in using line graphs relates to which axis represents which quantity. This choice has to do with which quantity is considered to be dependent on the other. For example, in the Penny Jar, the total number of pennies in the jar is dependent on the number of rounds. Therefore, the total number of pennies is called the *dependent variable*, and the number of rounds is the *independent variable*. The convention in creating tables and graphs is that values of the *independent variable* appear in the first column of the table and are graphed on the horizontal or *x*-axis. In equations, the independent variable is often designated as *x*. Values of the dependent variable appear in the second column of the table and are graphed on the vertical or *y*-axis. This variable is often designated as *y* in equations. In the situations in this unit, we have designated the dependent and independent variables as follows:

Situation	Independent variable (values on the horizontal axis)	Dependent variable (values on the vertical axis)
Temperature	Time	Temperature
Marathon racer (and other races)	Time	Speed
Penny Jar	Number of rounds	Total number of pennies
Cube towers	Number of floors	Number of windows
Plants	Time	Height

These choices are, in some sense, arbitrary. We choose "total number of pennies" to be the dependent variable because in this situation, we are usually figuring out the number of pennies, given the number of rounds. Therefore, we say that the number of pennies is dependent on the number of rounds, not vice versa. However, we *could* graph this situation in the nonconventional way, with number of pennies on the *x*-axis and round number on the *y*-axis. Students in Grade 4 do not know these conventions and may, quite sensibly, make a graph in this way. Compare the more conventional graph of a Penny Jar situation with the graph of the same situation with the axes reversed:

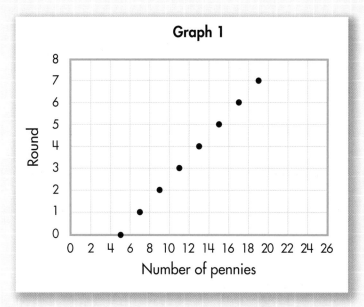

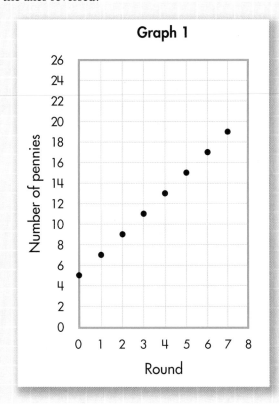

Both graphs correctly show the relationship between the number of pennies and the number of rounds. If graphing on opposite axes comes up in your class, help students read both graphs to see how both make sense. Then let students know that mathematicians usually choose one way to make graphs like this so that different graphs can be easily compared. Also tell them that you are choosing one way for the class to use, as indicated in the table shown on the previous page.

Line Graphs Show Values and How Those Values Are Changing

Once the conventions of creating line graphs are established, focus on how the graph shows both *values* and *changes in values*. The graph of temperatures in Moscow and Sydney shows particular values for temperatures. For example, the temperature in Syndey was about 75 degrees on February 4.

The graph also shows how the temperature is decreasing, increasing, or staying the same over certain periods. From September to December, the temperature in Moscow is generally decreasing.

An important focus of students' work is to learn how a line graph indicates change. In their work on the racer's story about the Boston Marathon in Session 1.2, students learn about associating the shape of sections of a graph with increasing, decreasing, or steady speed.

In the racer's story, students usually agree that these words and phrases describe a steady pace: *wheeled very fast, wheeled nice and steady, wheeled steadily, kept pushing slowly, ran my fastest, wheeled around slowly.* These parts of the story would be represented by sections of the graph that are horizontal—the speed is not increasing or decreasing. These are the phrases that most students think describe a change in pace: *slowed down a bit, pushed faster and faster, gradually slowing down, picked up the pace.* These parts of the story would be represented by sections of the graph that slant up or down, showing increase or decrease in speed. A few students distinguish between slowing down quickly and slowing down gradually by drawing a steep straight line or a less steep line.

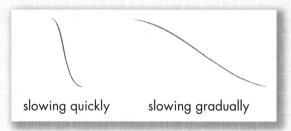

slowing quickly   slowing gradually

Students sometimes disagree about whether *stopped* is a steady speed or a change in speed. They can make good arguments on both sides. For example, one student said, "I put *stopped* in the change list because first he was moving, and then he stopped." This student is thinking about the change from *moving* to *stopping.* Another student said, "You might have been going fast before you went slowly, but going slowly is not a change in speed, so stopped is not a change in speed." This student is focusing on how *stopped* is a state of no speed. It would be represented by a horizontal line at the value of 0 on the graph. One interpretation of the racer's speed might look like the line graph below.

Sample Student Work

Sometimes students think that the graphs of speed are actually pictures of the course. That is, their graphs go up when the racer is going up a hill, or down when the racer is zooming downhill, even though the opposite would be more likely to show changing speed (slowing down as the racer goes uphill, speeding up going downhill). Here are examples of two students' interpretations of the motion graph on *Student Activity Book* page 5, The Motion Graph.

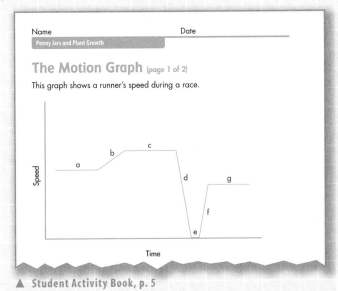

▲ **Student Activity Book, p. 5**

In the first story, the student correctly interprets the graph as representing speed over time. In the second, a different student interprets the changing slope as the trajectory of the race course.

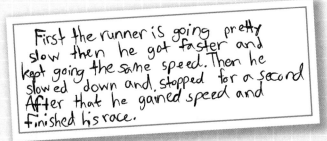

First the runner is going pretty slow then he got faster and kept going the same speed. Then he slowed down and stopped for a second After that he gained speed and finished his race.

Sample Student Work

He went slow on A and then he went up a hill on B to get to C wich is Strait. Then he went down the hill to D stopped at E for ice cream but it slowed him down, he went and stoped at g And won in 2nd place!

Sample Student Work

If some students in your class see a line graph as a picture of geography instead of as a representation of the changing values of the speed, work with them to think about times when they have gone up a hill or down a hill (running, on a bicycle, on skates, or whatever is in their experience). Then make a list of what the values of the speeds might be for a ride or run that goes like this: ride on a flat surface (e.g., 10 miles per hour), go up a steep hill getting more and more tired (e.g., 9 mph, 8 mph, 7 mph, 6 mph), go down the hill picking up speed (e.g., 6 mph, 7 mph, 8 mph, 9 mph, 10 mph), ride on a flat surface (e.g., 10 mph). Then sketch with students a graph of the speed of this ride by plotting these values, and talk through why the part of the graph that represents going up the steep hill has a line that goes down.

Situations with a Constant Rate of Change: Linear Functions

In this unit, students encounter a variety of situations in which two quantities are related. In Investigations 1 and 3, they work with change over time: speed, temperature, and the heights of plants. In these situations, students work with real data that vary over time. Some general trends can be predicted: a plant's height generally increases over time; the temperature in Moscow generally decreases from September to December. However, the values of the two quantities (e.g., time and temperature) are not related in a predictable way. That is, knowing the date in Moscow does not allow you to calculate the temperature.

In Investigation 2, students work with two situations of constant change—the Penny Jar and Windows and Towers—in which the two quantities in each situation are related in a predictable way. Once the starting amount and the rate of change are known, the total number of pennies can be calculated based on the number of rounds, and the total number of windows can be calculated based on the number of the building floors.

These two situations are *linear functions*. When these functions are graphed, the points fall in a straight line:

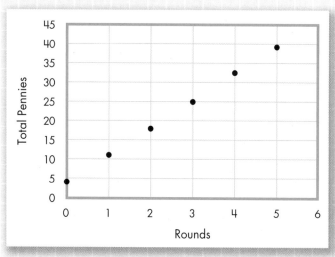

Because there can be only whole numbers of rounds and whole numbers of pennies in the Penny Jar, dots on the graph show the total number of pennies after each round. You can use a light line to "connect the dots" to show more clearly for students the way the total increases, but you should keep in mind that there are no actual values between points (that is, there is no Round 4.5, and there are never 6.5 pennies in the jar).

Although the term *linear function* is not used with students, they are grappling with what linear functions are and how they behave. They move from figuring out particular values of one of the quantities ("How many pennies will be in the jar after Round 8?") to determining general rules that relate the two quantities. They learn to take into account the starting amount and the rate of change in order to relate the two quantities. For example, if there are 3 pennies in the jar to start, and 10 pennies are added to the jar in each round, students might articulate this rule to find the total number of pennies after any round: Multiply the change, 10 pennies, by the number of rounds and add the 3 pennies that were in the jar at the beginning.

(Round number × 10) + 3 = Total number of pennies in the jar

Students also relate the total and the rate of change to solve "backward problems." For example, "Is it possible to have exactly 50 pennies in the jar, and, if so, after how many rounds?"

Number of Rounds	Total Number of Pennies
Start	6
1	11
2	16
3	21
4	26
5	31

At first, most students simply add on more rounds to see whether that number of pennies are ever in the jar. Encourage students to reason about what numbers of pennies are possible, as these two students do for a Penny Jar situation that starts with 6 pennies and adds 5 pennies each round:

"I think there will never be 50 because no matter how far you go, 6 + 5 will not equal 50 and 5 + 1 will not equal 50."

"No, you will never get 50. Every number in the rounds is a multiple of 5 plus 1. Each number ends in 1 or 6."

A few of the situations that students encounter have a value of 0 for the starting amount (e.g., Start with 0 pennies/Add 4 each round.). These are situations in which the two quantities are related as a direct proportion: The number of pennies in the jar and the number of the round form a constant ratio. In this case, the ratio of pennies to rounds is 4:1:

(Round number $\times$ 4) = Total number of pennies in the jar

See Algebra Connections In This Unit, page 18, for more information about linear functions and the special case of these functions where the starting amount is 0.

Throughout their work in Investigation 2, students describe and represent these linear functions by using and examining tables, graphs, and arithmetic expressions that use numbers and symbols. See **Teacher Note:** Representing a Constant Rate of Change, page 140. Also see **Dialogue Boxes:** Doubling or Not? page 156, and Comparing Penny Jars, page 158, for more information about how students consider the starting amount and the constant change as they work with these situations.

Note that throughout this unit, the phrase "situation of constant change" is used to designate a situation in which two variables are related by a constant rate of change. That is, for a certain amount of change in the value of one of the variables, there is always a certain amount of change in the value of the other variable (e.g., if the number of rounds increases by 1, the total number of pennies increases by 5).

Representing a Constant Rate of Change

In Investigation 2, students represent situations with a constant rate of change in several ways. They use their own representations, tables, graphs, words, and symbolic notation to show how the two quantities in a situation of constant change are related.

When students develop their own representations for the Penny Jar context, they are learning to pay attention to two elements: the starting number of pennies and a constant number of pennies added in each round. At first, students draw on representations that are already familiar to them, such as pictures, lists, tallies, bar graphs, or arithmetic expressions that use addition:

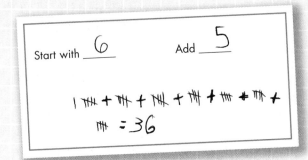

Jill's Work

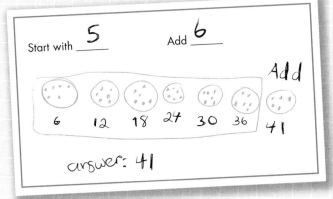

Derek's Work

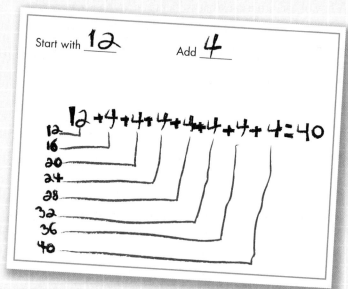

Jake's Work

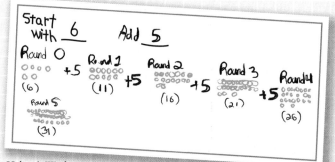

Helena's Work

Then students learn how to use conventional representations suited to showing the relationship between two quantities and how the relationship changes. As students represent and examine such relationships—using tables, line graphs, and arithmetic expressions involving multiplication—it is critical that they relate their work to the context, constantly connecting the numbers and symbols to their meanings.

Each representation—tables, line graphs, and arithmetic expressions—provides a different view into the meaning of the constant change situation, raising different learning issues and opportunities for students.

Tables

Tables provide an organized representation of data, showing how pairs of values are related. Consider this table of a Penny Jar situation that starts with 4 pennies and has 5 pennies added in each round:

Number of Rounds	Total Number of Pennies
Start with	4
1	9
2	14
3	19
4	24
5	29
6	34
7	39
10	

Students readily learn to complete tables by adding on. In this case, they see that at the beginning, the first column increases by 1 each time and the second column increases by 5. Because these addition patterns are so easy to see, students' attention is likely to be captured by these patterns; they may focus on extending the number pattern, but lose their sense of what the numbers mean in terms of the Penny Jar situation. See **Dialogue Box:** "I took a guess there was a pattern," page 154, for an example.

It is crucial to focus on the relationship of numbers in each row of the table, because it is the row that shows the relationship between the two quantities. You can point to a row of the table and ask, "Who can say a sentence about this row of the table? What information do the numbers in this row give us about the Penny Jar?" Looking at the relationship across a row of the table lays a foundation for making general statements about how the two quantities are related.

In this Investigation, the first columns of many tables do not include every consecutive value (the number of rounds in the Penny Jar or the number of floors in a tower), but rather skip some entries. Skipping values in the table helps

students think through the relationship between the two quantities rather than automatically adding on the amount of change. For example, in the table above, the number of rounds skips from 7 to 10. Instead of simply adding 5 to get the number of pennies for the next row of the table, students must pay attention to the number of rounds and its relationship to the total number of pennies. Initially, many students continue adding on to find the number of pennies in Round 10: "Round 8 would be 5 more, that's 44, then Round 9 is 49, and Round 10 is 54." Gradually, students learn to combine these steps, and as the jumps in the table get larger, they realize that the constant change is related by multiplication to the number of rounds.

When students compare two different functions, such as two Penny Jar situations, the table helps students see how the relative rates of change affect the relationship between the two situations. For an example of how students use a table to compare, see **Dialogue Box:** Comparing Penny Jars, page 158.

Line Graphs

Throughout this unit, students use and interpret graphs plotted on a coordinate grid that show the relationship between two quantities. Graphs provide another view of how the values of one quantity change in relationship to the values of another. In Investigations 1 and 3, the graphs show changes in temperature, speed, and plant height over time. In these Investigations, students learn how to interpret the meaning of the steepness of the graph and what that steepness indicates about the rate of the increases or decreases. In Investigation 2, students notice that the points on their graphs of the Penny Jar and Windows and Towers situations always fall in straight lines. As one quantity changes by a certain amount, the other quantity changes by a corresponding amount. For example, in the Penny Jar situation shown in the table above, as the round number increases by 1, the total number of pennies increases by 5. This is true whether the round number is increasing from 10 to 11, or from 32 to 33, or from 1000 to 1001. Because every horizontal change of 1 results in a vertical change of 5, the slope or steepness of the graph is the same at any point, and the points on the resulting graph fall in a straight line.

Graphs are particularly useful when comparing functions, as students do with the Penny Jar. These comparisons highlight the two components of these situations—the starting amount and the amount of constant change. Here are the three situations that students consider:

- One function in which the dependent variable (total number of pennies) that has a lower starting value than in the other but increases at a faster rate, resulting in graph lines that cross each other.

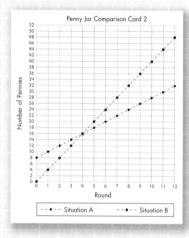

- Two functions in which the dependent variables start close together but increase at different rates, resulting in graph lines that start near the same point, and then get farther and farther apart.

- Two functions in which the dependent variables start at different values, but increase at the same rate, resulting in graph lines that are parallel.

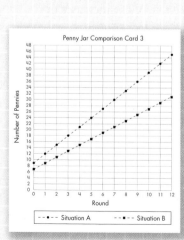

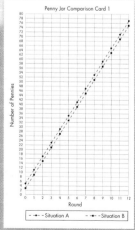

Words and Symbols

In situations with a constant rate of change, the value of one quantity can be determined if the value of the other quantity is given. Students develop rules for finding the total number of pennies for any round in a Penny Jar situation and for the number of windows in each of the four tower situations.

At first, it is important that students articulate their rules in words:

"I multiplied the round number by 5, and then added 4 because that was the number of pennies in the jar at the beginning."

Gradually their words can be transformed into shorter forms:

Round number $\times$ 5 + 4

When students become comfortable with this form of generalization and can explain why their general rule works, symbolic notation can be introduced as a short way to say "any number":

$(R \times 5) + 4$ or $(n \times 5) + 4$ or $4 + (n \times 5)$

Move back and forth between words and symbols so that students do not lose track of what these letters mean in the context of the Penny Jar or windows situations.

Some students realize that by using a letter to stand for each quantity, they can create expressions for *any* Penny Jar situation. For example, if n is the number of rounds, a is the number of pennies added each time, and s is the starting number of pennies, then an equation for finding the total number of pennies in any Penny Jar situation is

total number of pennies $= (n \times a) + s$

It is not expected that all students become fluent with using letters to represent variables in Grade 4, but students should be able to use words and arithmetic expressions to express a general rule for a particular Penny Jar or windows situation.

Teacher Note

Height or Change in Height?

In Investigation 3, students return to situations in which change does not occur at a constant rate. Like the speed and temperature graphs in Investigation 1, the graphs of plant heights show varying change: Sometimes the plants grow faster, sometimes slower, and sometimes they stop growing.

It is typical for fourth-grade students to need time and experience to sort out how their graphs show height and how they show change in height. In this Investigation, the teacher must help students interpret which features of the graph indicate height and which features indicate change in height.

Here is an example:

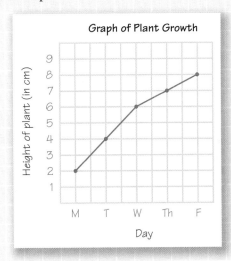

One way of reading this graph is to look at the height of the plant each day. On Monday, the plant was 2 centimeters tall; on Tuesday it was 4 centimeters tall; on Wednesday it was 6 centimeters tall; and so forth. These values could also be represented in a table:

Day	Height of plant (in cm)
Monday	2
Tuesday	4
Wednesday	6
Thursday	7
Friday	8

Another kind of information that is represented in both the graph and the table is the rate at which the height of the plant changes. From Monday to Wednesday, the height increases at a constant rate. From Wednesday to Friday, the height increases at a constant, but slower, rate. The change in rate of growth can be seen in the slope of the graph. From Wednesday to Friday, the graph is not as steep as it is from Monday to Wednesday, indicating less growth per day. This change in the rate of growth also appears in the table. If we look at the differences in height from one day to the next, we can see that the rate of change is greater from Monday to Wednesday than from Wednesday to Friday:

Day	Height of plant (in cm)	
Monday	2	2
Tuesday	4	2
Wednesday	6	1
Thursday	7	1
Friday	8	

In this unit, students are learning how to distinguish the way a graph represents values from the way a graph represents changes in those values. Difficulties in distinguishing between how a graph shows height and how it shows *change* in height most often come up in two situations. The first situation is the interpretation of a horizontal part of a graph of height over time (e.g., the part of this graph labeled A):

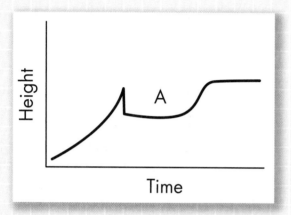

This part of the graph shows no change in height, but some students interpret it as "growing at a steady rate." Consider one student's response to this example from the End-of-Unit Assessment:

the plant was ok then it was growing faster then my brother droped it then it was growing at a normal pace the fast again the a steardy speed

Sample Student Work

On most of this graph, the student has correctly interpreted the steepness of the line as representing rate of growth, but the student then incorrectly interprets the horizontal part of the graph as representing a steady rate of growth rather than no growth. It seems that at one moment, the student sees the line as representing the plant's height; the next moment, the plant's rate of growth.

Students may also have difficulty interpreting a decreasing rate of growth. That is, the height of the plant is still increasing, but increasing at a slower rate, as in the growth from Wednesday to Friday in the first example. Students sometimes think that to show a decrease in the rate of growth, the graph would slant downward. It is worth spending time discussing how a graph of height over time shows *decreasing height* (as when a part of the plant breaks off) and how it shows a *decreasing rate of growth*.

As part of the introduction to the activity in Session 3.3 and the discussion at the end of that session, help students think through how the graphs represent height and change in height by asking questions such as:

If the plant is 5 centimeters tall at this point on the graph, is it taller or shorter at this point? At this point?

If the graph goes up, what does that mean? If the graph goes down, what does that mean?

What is happening in the portion of the graph from here to here? Is the height increasing more quickly or more slowly than in this part of the graph?

What does this horizontal portion of the graph mean? Why doesn't this horizontal portion of the graph mean "growing steadily"?

End-of-Unit Assessment

Problems 1–3

Benchmarks addressed:

Benchmark 1: Connect tables and graphs of change over time to each other and to the situations they represent.

Benchmark 3: Describe how a graph shows change: where the rate of change is increasing, decreasing, or remaining constant; and how differences in steepness represent differences in the rate of change.

In order to meet the benchmarks, students' work should show that they can:

- Determine which of two graphs represents faster or slower change;

- Describe parts of a graph as representing increasing change or no change;

- Use the relative steepness of parts of a graph to represent slower or faster change;

- Match the parts of a story about growth to those parts of a graph that represent that story.

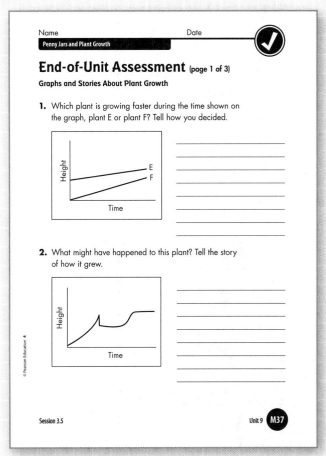

▲ Resource Masters, M37

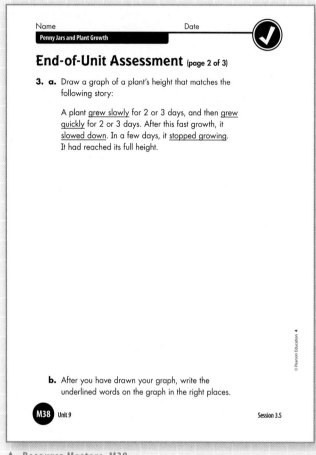

▲ Resource Masters, M38

Meeting the Benchmarks

The first three End-of-Unit Assessment problems focus on interpreting graphs of plant growth and matching graphs and stories.

Students who meet the benchmarks correctly determine that Plant F is growing faster than Plant E in Problem 1. They write a story for Problem 2 that describes a sequence of growth with five parts: increasing height, decreased height, no growth, increasing height, and no growth. Some students also note that the second increase is slower than the first increase. Finally, they sketch and label a graph for Problem 3 with sections that correctly match the four underlined phrases in the story. In particular, their graph distinguishes

between "grew slowly" and "grew quickly" by following a less steep section of the graph with a steeper section.

Here are examples of good explanations from student work for Problem 1:

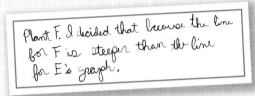

Sabrina's Work

F is because if you look closely, F slants up steeper than E slants up.

Ursula's Work

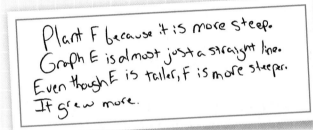

Richard's Work

Plant F because in height it has gone up more.

Steve's Work

The first three students refer specifically to the relative steepness of the two lines. While the fourth student does not mention steepness, this student observes that over the same amount of time, Plant F's height has increased more than Plant E's, which is another way of describing a greater rate of change.

In both Problem 2 and 3, good responses indicate that students associate an upward slanting portion of the graph with increasing height, a straight portion of the graph with no growth, and, in Problem 2, a drop in the graph with decreasing height. In Problem 3, they differentiate "grew slowly," "grew quickly," and "slowed down" by showing relative steepness in these parts of their graph. In particular, they do not confuse "slowed down" with a decrease in height, but draw this part of the graph as less steep, but still increasing. Drawing the part of the graph for "slowed down" is typically the most difficult idea in these first three problems. If a student has good responses to all parts of these problems except this one, the student has demonstrated a good understanding of graphing change and has met the benchmarks for these problems.

In a good response to Problem 2, students distinguish between growing slowly and growing quickly, describe the sudden decrease in height, and describe plateaus in growth:

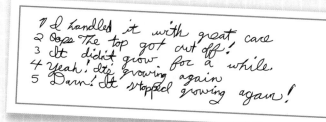

Amelia's Work

Enrique's Work

In the second student's description of the graph's beginning, the student refers to the care of the plant rather than describing the growth. However, it seems likely that this student meant that the plant was growing well because of good care. From the rest of the student's response to this

question, as well as very good responses to Problems 1 and 3, it is clear that this student meets the benchmarks for these tasks.

The third student's work is less elaborate but still shows an understanding of the basic ideas:

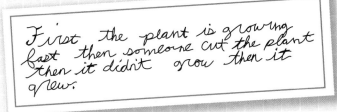

Marisol's Work

Some students write about the possible causes of faster and slower growth, but their responses make it clear that they understand what the graph shows:

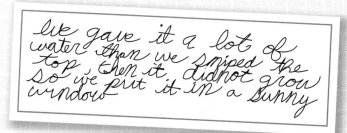

Alejandro's Work

A good response to Problem 3 shows a line that is less steep for "grew slowly," then steeper to show "grew quickly," then less steep again to show "slowed down," and then horizontal to show "stopped growing." For example:

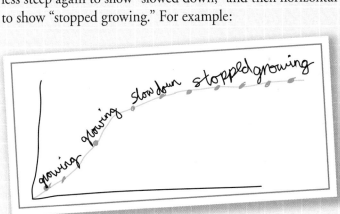

Emaan's Work

Partially Meeting the Benchmarks

Common reasons for students to only partially meet the benchmarks for Problems 1–3 include confusion about how to represent "growing slowly" or "slowing down" on a graph of plant height, and confusion about the interpretation of a horizontal line on the graph. Some students interpret a horizontal line to mean *no change in the rate of growth* rather than *no change in the height of the plant*. Even though on some parts of these problems they have correctly interpreted the steepness of the line as representing rate of growth, they look at the horizontal line as if it represents a steady rate of growth. This would be correct if the graph represented rate of growth over time instead of height over time. It is as if they are moving back and forth between interpreting the line graph as representing height and interpreting it as representing rate of growth. On Problem 2, this results in correct interpretations of all parts of the graph except for the horizontal portions:

> the plant was ok then it was growing faster then my brother droped it then it was growing at a normal pace then fast then agian a steady speed

Terrell's Work

In this example of Problem 3, a student who wrote a correct story for Problem 2 sketched the following graph:

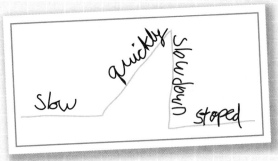

Damian's Work

The student first graphs "grew slowly" as a horizontal line, as if this were a graph of speed over time. Then, the student uses a line slanting upward to show "grew quickly," as if to show increasing height. The student uses a vertical line to show "slowed down." This indicates that the student may have lost track of the x-axis as representing time, showing a decrease in speed using only the vertical axis. This same student correctly interpreted the vertical line in Problem 2 as a sudden decrease in height ("we broke the top"). Although this student clearly has some important ideas in place, as these ideas are not yet entirely firm.

Students may also have a partially correct answer on Problem 1. A student may correctly choose F as the plant that grew faster but have an incomplete explanation. For example, this student's explanation includes important observations—in particular, that Plant F grew more even though it started at a lower height. However, the student's statement that "they both end up the same" is unclear because the plants do not end up at the same height. The student may simply mean that the plants' heights are closer at the end than at the beginning:

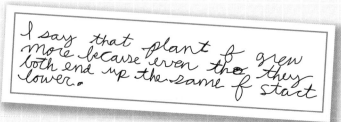

> I say that plant f grew more because even tho they both end up the same f start lower.

Ramona's Work

Not Meeting the Benchmarks

Some students who do not correctly answer Problem 1 choose Plant F, but do not have an explanation that refers to the relative steepness of the lines:

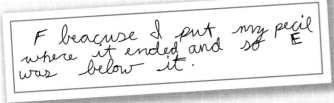

Yuki's Work

Other students choose Plant E:

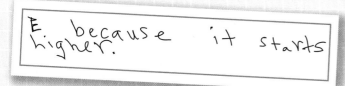

Abdul's Work

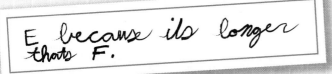

Benson's Work

On Problems 2 and 3, students who do not meet the benchmarks do not write a reasonable story to match the graph and do not draw a graph that matches the words in the story. Here are two examples for Problem 3:

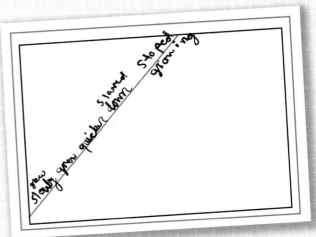

Noemi's Work

Venetta's Work

The first response treats the line as if its only function is to indicate a sequence of events rather than to show any change in height or change in rate of growth. The second student does not distinguish between "grew slow" and "grew fast," and does not distinguish between "slowed down" and "stopped growing."

Problems 4–5

Benchmarks addressed:

Benchmark 1: Connect tables and graphs to each other and to the situations they represent.

Benchmark 4: Take into account the starting amount and the amount of change in describing and comparing situations of constant change.

Benchmark 5: In a situation of constant change, write rules (using words or arithmetic expressions) to determine the value of one quantity, given the value of the other.

In order to meet the benchmarks, students' work should show that they can:

• Correctly complete the table;

• Write an arithmetic expression for the number of acorns on Day 100 that correctly takes into account the starting amount and the constant change.

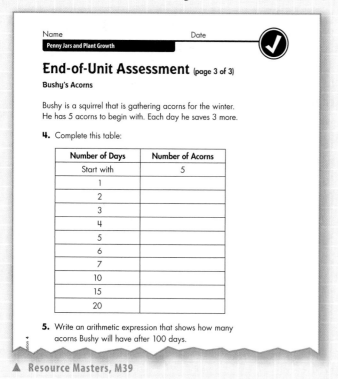

▲ **Resource Masters, M39**

Meeting the Benchmarks

The final two problems of the assessment focus on a situation of constant change.

Students who meet the benchmarks complete all of the rows of the table correctly and write an arithmetic expression that correctly gives the number of acorns for Day 100.

Number of Days	Number of Acorns
Start with	5
1	8
2	11
3	14
4	17
5	20
6	23
7	26
10	35
15	50
20	65

Nadeem's Work

Arithmetic expressions might be written in one or two steps, for example:

$$(3 \times 100) + 5 = 305$$

$$5 + (3 \times 100) = 305$$

$$100 \times 3 = 300$$
$$300 + 5 = 305$$

A few students use the values they have already calculated in the table to figure out Day 100. For example, one student thought through the task this way:

$100 - 20 = 80$ rounds more to get to 100

$80 \times 3 = 240$ (the number of acorns in 80 more rounds)

$240 + 65 = 305$ (add the number of acorns in the first 20 rounds and the number of acorns in 80 more rounds)

If a student makes a minor arithmetic error in one row of the table but then correctly calculates other rows based on that error, the student has met the benchmark. Similarly, if a student makes an arithmetic mistake in one of the final three rows, but correctly calculates the other two, as this student did, the student meets the benchmark:

Number of Days	Number of Acorns
Start with	5
1	8
2	11
3	14
4	17
5	20
6	23
7	26
10	29
15	50
20	65

Tonya's Work

Partially Meeting the Benchmarks

Some students fill out the last three rows of the table incorrectly, continuing the +3 sequence as if figuring out the number of acorns for 8, 9, and 10 days, instead of 10, 15, and 20 days. However, if these students write correct arithmetic expressions for the number of acorns after 100 days, they demonstrate that they do know how to take into account the starting amount and the constant change. They have partially met the benchmarks.

Other students incorrectly double the number of acorns for Day 5 to get the number of acorns for Day 10. Using this method, they calculate 40 acorns for Day 10 instead of 35 acorns. Students might then double this amount again to find the number of acorns for Day 20. However, they

give a correct arithmetic expression for 100 acorns, showing that they do know how to take into account the starting amount and the constant change, so they partially meet the benchmarks.

Not Meeting the Benchmarks

Some students ignore the starting amount and work only with multiples of 3, both in the table and in the arithmetic expression:

Number of Days	Number of Acorns
Start with	5
1	8
2	11
3	14
4	17
5	20
6	23
7	26
10	30
15	45
20	60

5. Write an arithmetic expression that shows how many acorns Bushy will have after 100 days.

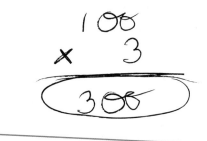

Sample Student Work

Other students confuse the meanings of the numbers in this situation. This student fills out the table correctly through Day 7, then fills out Days 10, 15, and 20 as if the increase in each instance is 15 acorns. This is the correct amount of increase between 10 and 15 days and between 15 and 20 days (5 days × 3 acorns per day), but it is not the correct increase between 7 and 10 days (which should be 3 days × 3 acorns per day, or 9 acorns). It is probable that the student has incorrectly calculated the increase between 7 and 10 days as 5 acorns per day, carrying on this increase of 15 without noticing that the jumps are now 5 days instead of 3 days.

This response could place the student in the category of partially meeting the benchmarks if the student's work on Problem 5 made clear that the student understood the meaning of the starting amount and the amount of constant change. However, this student's arithmetic demonstrates that the student is not keeping track of the relationship between the number of acorns and the number of days. The student calculates that there are 80 days remaining, then multiplies 80 by 15, as if there were 15 acorns for each of 80 days. The student may be thinking about the 15 that was used incorrectly in the table, and so now thinks that the increase each day is 15 acorns. All in all, the student confuses the relationship between the starting amount, the amount of constant change, the number of days, and the total number of acorns.

Number of Days	Number of Acorns
Start with	5
1	8
2	11
3	14
4	17
5	20
6	23
7	26
10	41
15	56
20	71

5. Write an arithmetic expression that shows how many acorns Bushy will have after 100 days.

$$100 - 20 = 80$$
$$80 \times 15 = 1200$$
$$\times 0 = 800 \quad 800 + 400 = 1200$$
$$\times 5 = 400$$

Sample Student Work

How Is the Temperature Changing?

During Session 1.1, students are discussing the shape of the graph for Moscow and Sydney on *Student Activity Book* page 3.

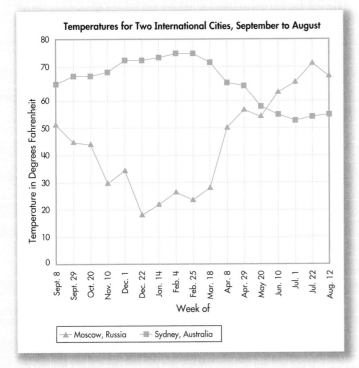

Teacher: Let's look at the Moscow graph. Who can show me with your hand what the first part of the graph looks like?

Enrique: It goes down, and it's a little jagged.

Marisol: I think it's like this. [Marisol holds her left hand diagonally, slanting down and to her right.]

Emaan: It's a diagonal going down. [Emaan shows this with his arm.]

Teacher: How is the temperature changing?

Jake: The temperature drops down about every week. It gets colder and colder. And sometimes it gets slightly warmer.

Steve: But the temperature keeps changing. There are lots of spikes.

Teacher: So overall would you say it is getting warmer or colder?

Ramona: A little of both, but mostly colder until around December.

Lucy: The lowest it goes is around 20 or 18 degrees. Then it starts going up again.

Teacher: Then what happens?

Ursula: Overall it is going higher. The line has jags and goes down sometimes. But it goes farther up than it is going down. It goes down a little and more up.

Teacher: What does that mean about the temperature in Moscow after December?

Yuki: It climbs up and up until July. Then it's about as warm as in Sydney.

Teacher: What about the graph for Sydney?

Richard: It doesn't change as much.

Amelia: It's like it's steady and it's around the 60s and 70s.

Lucy: But it's not steady, because it still goes up and down a little.

Teacher: What do you think? Does Sydney have a steady temperature? Who can say something about that and show us evidence on the graph for what you are saying?

Alejandro: It's kind of steady for the first half. It's just changing a little bit. See, here from the beginning to February 25. But then it goes down more.

The teacher helps students describe the overall trend of the graph with gestures and language. Many of the students are noticing the overall shape of parts of the graph as increasing, decreasing, or staying the same, despite fluctuations. By asking questions such as, "How is the temperature changing?" and "What does that mean about the temperature in Moscow after December?" the teacher makes sure that students are connecting the shape of the graph with its meaning in terms of temperature.

"I took a guess that there was a pattern"

In Session 2.2, students work in pairs on *Student Activity Book* pages 17–18. Noemi and Yuki are completing the table using a pattern they found in the number sequence. This pattern works successfully for them for round 10, but leads them to an incorrect answer for rounds 15 and 20. The teacher asks them to explain their work.

1. a. Fill in the numbers for a Penny Jar situation:
Start with __6__ pennies. Add __5__ pennies each round.

b. Complete this table:

Number of Rounds	Total Number of Pennies
Start with	6
1	11
2	16
3	21
4	26
5	31
6	36
7	41
10	56
15	71
20	86

Noemi and Yuki's Work

Noemi: We figured it out because there is a pattern.

Yuki: It goes 6, 1, 6, 1, 6, 1. If it goes to round 21, it would be 91, because round 20 is 86.

Noemi: We just figured out the ones column first, because it's a 6 or a 1. Then we figured out the other number.

Teacher: How did you determine the amount for round 10?

Noemi: Because 5 times 3 is 15. And it ends in a 6 because the even rounds end with 6.

Yuki: We added the 15 to the 41.

Teacher: Why did you do 5 times 3? Tell me what the 5 means and what the 3 means.

Yuki: Because it skips 3. Like, it goes round 7, and then 8, 9, 10. So there are three more rounds to get to round 10. And each round is 5 pennies.

Teacher: OK, each round is 5 pennies and it's 3 rounds from round 7 to round 10. What about round 15?

Yuki: I took a guess that there was a pattern.

Noemi: Yeah, we did the same thing because we found the pattern. So we just add 15 to round 10 is 71, and then add 15 to find round 20 is 86.

Yuki and Noemi have noticed that the table jumps, but after determining a way to work through the first jump in the table, they apply this same method to any jump in the table. The teacher asks them how many rounds there are from round 7 to round 10.

Yuki: Three rounds. So it skips 3 times 5.

Teacher: How many rounds are there from round 10 to round 15?

Yuki: Five.

Teacher: Does your same method work this time, since there are 5 rounds instead of 3 rounds?

Noemi: So it's not 71? There's not a pattern?

Teacher: I understood you when you explained that there are 3 rounds with 5 pennies in each round to get from round 7 to round 10. But now you say that there are 5 more rounds to get to round 15. How many pennies are added in each of those 5 rounds from round 10 to round 15?

Yuki: Five pennies. Oh, so it would be 5 times 5, for each round.

Teacher: And what do you mean by 5 times 5? You said one of the 5s is five pennies?

Noemi: Five rounds and 5 pennies each time. Five times 5 is 25. But, what is the pattern?

Yuki: I don't know if it's a pattern. But it goes by 5 for every round.

Noemi: Oh, it's 81! Oh, so for round 20 I could do that same thing. Because another 5 rounds go by, so it's another 25 pennies. So it's 106, because I added 25 to the number for 15 rounds.

It is important that students develop the habit of seeing and describing patterns throughout their work in mathematics. Patterns are useful in revealing underlying mathematical structures and relationships. However, simply finding patterns for the sake of finding patterns, without thinking about what a particular pattern indicates about the mathematics, can lead students in unproductive directions. For example, when using tables, students sometimes get lost in the number patterns that are a result of a constant change without connecting those patterns to the situation. Throughout students' work with tables, continually ask them what the numbers mean and how they relate to the context. Ask students to articulate what they are trying to find out in terms of the situation. Ask questions, as this teacher does, such as "Tell me what the 5 means and what the 3 means."

Dialogue Box

Doubling or Not?

During Session 2.3, these students are discussing whether doubling the number of pennies in round 10 will tell them the number of pennies in round 20. The teacher decides to focus everyone on the Penny Jar situation below.

Start with 5 pennies.
Add 6 pennies each round.

Teacher: Who had a way to figure out the number of pennies in round 20?

Richard: I did twenty 6s, that's 120. Then I added on the starting amount, so it's 125.

Amelia: I already knew that ten 6s is 60, so double that and it's 120.

Teacher: OK, slow down a little so everyone can follow you. Why did you double 60?

Amelia: So you have 6 pennies in each round, right? So in 10 rounds, that's 10 × 6. So for 20 rounds, just double it. 60 and 60 is 120.

Teacher: So Richard said 125 pennies, and you are saying 120 pennies.

Amelia: Oh, yeah, no—so me and Derek thought it was 120 at first. Then Jill and Duante had 125, so we realized we didn't add on the start number, so it's 125.

Teacher: Did anyone else do something that didn't work at first?

Andrew: Yeah. We doubled 65 and we got 130.

Teacher: Why did you double 65?

Andrew: In 10 rounds, you have 65 pennies, so we just doubled that for 20 rounds.

Teacher: And now you think that doesn't work? That's one of our questions. Can you double round 10 to get round 20? Who has something to say about this question?

Venetta: All you have to do is look at round 10 and double what it is and then just subtract the starting number.

Jake: If you had 65, you can't double the start number because you can only use it once, so you would probably have to do 65 and then minus 5 and then plus another 65. You could do 60 plus 65.

The teacher records Venetta's and Jake's methods on the board.

Teacher: So Venetta and Jake are using doubling, but then each of them has another step that has to do with the start number. Venetta doubled round 10, and then subtracted the start number. Jake first subtracted the start number from the number of pennies in round 10, then added 65. Do their methods work?

Enrique: You have to subtract the start. If you just double 65, you're going past your answer.

Teacher: What's 65 plus 65?

Various students: 130.

Teacher: That's not the right answer. Why not?

Ramona: You're doubling the start number.

Teacher: So, let's see if we can understand what you're saying, Ramona. Here's a picture for round 10. I'll use Richard's method. In the jar we had 5 pennies at the beginning and then we had 10 rounds with 6 pennies in each round.

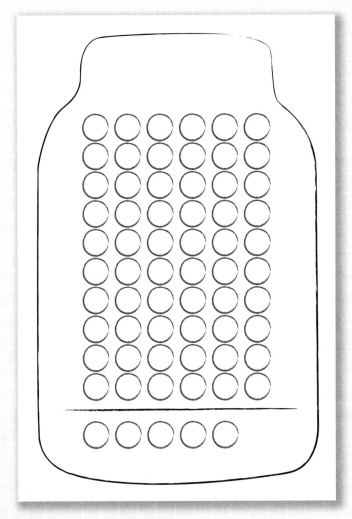

Teacher: Can someone use this picture to explain why you can't just double this number of pennies in round 10 to get the number for round 20?

Marisol: It's like what Enrique said. You'll go past your answer. Look.

Marisol draws a second Penny Jar next to the teacher's drawing.

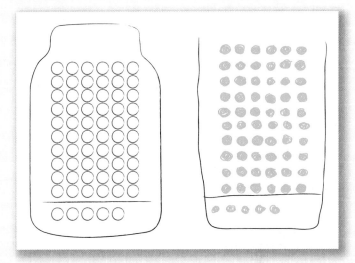

Andrew: Oh! It's like you'd go start, start. You can only have the start amount once. If you double it, you have it twice.

While many of the students are making good arguments about why the number of pennies in round 20 is not double the number in round 10, the teacher knows that not all students are following these arguments. The teacher thinks that some students may be agreeing that doubling does not work in this case because they know the correct answer for round 20 is 125 pennies, not because they understand why doubling does not work. Because the class is familiar with an array representation, the teacher brings in this representation to help students better visualize what is going on when the number of pennies is doubled.

Dialogue Box

Comparing Penny Jars

In Session 2.7, students are describing and comparing the situations on Penny Jar Comparison Card 2. The teacher puts a completed table showing the values for these two penny jars on the board and then asks what students notice about how the total number of pennies changes in the two jars.

Round	Situation A: Total Number of Pennies	Situation B: Total Number of Pennies
Starts with	8	0
1	10	4
2	12	8
3	14	12
4	16	16
5	18	20
6	20	24
7	22	28
10	28	40
15	38	60
20	48	80

Anna: Penny Jar A had 8 pennies more than Jar B. And then at the end, Jar B has a lot more than A.

Tonya: Penny Jar B catches up.

Derek: 4 is more than 2, so Jar B is going to have more.

Luke: It's bigger steps, so it will catch up.

Venetta: Jar A is slower than Jar B because of the 4. Jar B quickly catches up and passes.

Nadeem: By round 3, Jar B is just 2 away.

Amelia: On round 4, they both have 16 pennies. And after that, Jar B has more.

Sabrina: Jar A was winning at first and then Jar B won because it got more each time.

Ramona: And also, the difference between 4 and 2 is 2.

Teacher: What do you mean, the difference between 4 and 2? Why is that important?

Ramona: The difference between what you put in is 2.

Teacher: And why is the 2 important?

Marisol: The difference keeps counting by 2s.

Andrew: Round 1, Jar A is in the lead with 6 more and round 2, it's 4 more, and round 3 it's 2 more.

Yuson: And then it's 0!

The teacher records what Andrew and Yuson are saying like this:

Round	Situation A: Total Number of Pennies	Situation B: Total Number of Pennies	
Starts with	8	0	
1	10	4	6
2	12	8	4
3	14	12	2
4	16	16	0
5	18	20	
6	20	24	
7	22	28	
10	28	40	
15	38	60	
20	48	80	

Emaan: It keeps on. If you look at the 2s thing, it keeps on going.

Teacher: So, if you look at it going forward, what is happening?

Richard: They are tied on round 4 and then it goes up by 2 the other way.

Teacher: What do you mean by it goes the other way?

Richard: Jar B goes up by 2 now. First it's 0, then 2, then 4, 6, and it keeps going.

Teacher: What about the graph of these two Penny Jars? What does that look like?

Noemi: The two graph lines get closer together and then they go apart.

LaTanya: It will look like an X. Once they've crossed over, they'll go wider and wider.

Teacher: And what does that mean?

Steve: First one has more. Then they have the same for just a minute. Then the other one has more.

Bill: Jar B will have more and more. In the future, Jar B will have a lot more pennies.

The students are noticing an important feature of the comparison between Penny Jar A and Penny Jar B. Although Jar A starts out with 8 more pennies, Jar B accumulates pennies at a higher rate (4 pennies per round) than Jar A (2 pennies per round). Ramona and Marisol point out that Jar B accumulates 2 more pennies per round than Jar A. Over time, this accumulation of 2 more per round means that the total number of pennies in Jar B equals and then overtakes the number of pennies in Jar A. The teacher records the differences that students notice on the table and also draws their attention to how they can see the increasing difference on the graph.

Dialogue Box

Rules for the Double Tower

In Session 2.8, students have found rules for the number of windows in the different types of cube tower. Several different rules have been written on the chart for the double tower. The teacher asks several students to explain their rules.

She first points at one of the rules on the chart:
Floors × 6 + 2

Teacher: I'd like to see if the class agrees with each of these rules. Some of them look different from one another. What about this one? Who can talk about how and why this rule works? Come up here and show us on this double tower.

Alejandro: That was ours. Our rule is to multiply the number of floors by 6 and then add 2. Two is for the skylight.

Teacher: You and quite a few other people said multiply by 6. I want to know why is this number 6? Who can use this tower to explain and show us what you mean?

Ursula: Because there are two on the front, two on the back, and one on that side and that side. [She points to one floor of the tower and shows where all the windows are on that floor.]

Ursula uses the everyday language of "sides" of a building to refer to the faces of the cube tower.

Venetta: As many times as there are sides, is how many sides there are.

Teacher: OK, how many sides there are. I hear the word "sides" being used in a lot of ways. Venetta, can you clarify what you mean, and why you think Alejandro is saying "number of floors multiplied by 6" to get the number of windows?

Venetta: Well, you have to count the windows on one side of the building and then multiply it by the number or add that number—how many sides there are—that many times. Like on this one . . .

Teacher: Come up and show us.

Venetta: OK. Like on this one. [She picks up a double tower with 10 floors.] There are six sides: 1, 2, 3, 4, 5, 6 [she runs her finger down each column of cube faces]. There are 10 on each side, so add 10 six times. Ten plus 10 plus 10 plus 10 plus 10 plus 10, and then you have to add 2 skylights.

Teacher: Let's say this tower isn't 10 floors high anymore. I've just got this enormous building, and I know it's a certain number of floors. Would your rule still work for this enormous number?

Steve: Yes, you just do like that number times 6 because there's 6 windows, and it's that number for every floor.

Lucy: And add the 2 for the skylights.

Teacher: Someone wrote this rule: "Count the windows." Will it work, even for my enormous building?

Steve: It will work, but it will take a really long time to count.

Teacher: Yes, it could be difficult to count. There's also sometimes a problem with counting when you're counting a big quantity. It's easy to lose track or to miscount by 1 or 2. Some of these rules can more easily give us an accurate answer. Here's an interesting rule.

Ramona has written:

$$8$$
$$8 + 8 - 2 = 14$$
$$14 + 8 - 2 = 20$$
$$20 + 8 - 2 = 26$$
$$26 + 8 - 2 = 32$$

and you just keep going

Teacher: Let's see what the class thinks about this one. What's going on, and how does it work?

Bill: It's going up 6 and minusing 2.

Helena: No, it's going up 8 then minusing 2.

Teacher: Hmmm. Why would someone add 8 then subtract 2? Where do you see 8 on this tower?

Noemi: Because 8 minus 2 would be 6 and it's the same as, um, . . . [Noemi trails off]

Andrew: On the sides and on the top.

Teacher: Can you show us what you mean by "on the sides and on the top"?

Andrew points to the top floor of the tower, showing 6 windows around the faces of the tower and the 2 skylights on top.

Andrew: So then you have to subtract the 2 skylights on top.

Teacher: Who wrote this one? . . . Ramona, can you explain how you were thinking about it?

Ramona: It's if you have 8 all together on one floor at the beginning, and then if you put 1 on top, you subtract the 2 you cover up. You have to minus those 2 and they go on top.

Enrique: But doesn't that seem a little weird? If you had 2 skylights on top, would you add another floor and take out the skylights?

Ramona: Actually, if you were building up from the bottom, it goes like this—the floor with the skylights, then you move that one up and put another one underneath.

Teacher: I know this isn't how a real building would be built. But what Ramona is saying is that her rule works to get the number of windows if you think of it that way. The first floor has 8 windows, including the

2 skylights. Then if you put the next floor underneath (she demonstrates with the cubes), you're putting on 8 more windows, but you're covering up 2. So add 8, subtract 2.

Students in this class have come up with a variety of rules. The teacher started with the rule, "Floors × 6 + 2" because many of the students in the class thought about the double tower in this way. The teacher wants to establish the correspondence between each part of the rule and its physical counterpart in the tower. Venetta shows one way of thinking about "floors × 6." She sees each column of windows in the double tower as having the same number of windows as floors; since there are 6 columns, the total number of windows (without skylights) is the number of floors multiplied by 6. You may have students who picture "floors × 6" differently when they look at the tower. They think of 6 windows around each floor of the tower, and then multiply the number of windows per floor by the number of floors.

The teacher also brings up one student's idea to "count the windows." The teacher spends a short time on this idea in order to bring up why creating a rule for any number of floors is valuable. Finally, the teacher turns to Ramona's rule, which can be called a "recursive rule" because determining the number of windows for each floor depends on knowing the number of windows in the previous floor. Students often come up with such rules; these can also be valuable for thinking through how parts of a rule relate to the situation. In this case, the teacher noticed that Ramona was visualizing the double tower in a different way and thought it would be valuable for students to go through a different way of thinking about the structure of the tower. Sometimes students who think about the first floor as having 8 windows and all subsequent floors having 6, as Ramona does, write a rule something like this:

Go 1 floor down. Multiply that number of floors times 6. Then add 8.

In other words, the number of windows in a double tower of 10 is $(9 \times 6) + 8$.

Which Graphs Are Straight?

In Session 3.4, the class is discussing all of the different situations that they have encountered in this unit. They have made a list on the board and are considering how the graphs of these situations are the same or different. Some students have brought up the idea that some graphs are straight and some have curves. In this part of the discussion, the teacher pursues this point.

> The wheelchair racer in the marathon
>
> Temperature in Sydney and Moscow
>
> Penny Jars
>
> Windows on cube buildings
>
> Plants

Teacher: Terrell and Helena are both saying that some graphs are straight and some are curved. Can you say more about this idea?

Terrell: I don't mean straight like up and down. I mean any kind of straight. It could be slanted.

Teacher: Why do your Penny Jar graphs look like this [shows a slightly slanted line with an arm] as opposed to the way the temperature graphs look?

Ramona: It's not really rapidly changing. You don't have big numbers. It's small numbers going up, up, up. It won't go down. The numbers increase; they won't get small.

Teacher: These numbers are increasing, aren't they? The temperature graph both increases and decreases. But Terrell and Helena said something about straight or curved. Which of these are going to be straight lines? I don't mean straight like horizontal [shows with an arm]. As Terrell said, it could be slanted this much or this much [shows slanting lines with an arm].

Noemi: The Penny Jar.

Teacher: Do people agree with that? . . . [many students indicate agreement by showing thumbs up] . . . And why is that?

Anna: Because you start with a certain amount and then you might get 2 each day, but it doesn't change; you don't start getting 4 a day.

Alejandro: I think it's because since you only put the same number over and over again, it doesn't go higher like it would if you put a 3, then a 4, and then a 6.

Teacher: How about the wheelchair racer in the marathon?

Luke: It won't be straight because he slows down and stops and speeds up. It's not going to be steady.

Yuson: He's not just speeding up the same amount and the same amount forever. He gets slower and faster and slower and faster, but the Penny Jar is just, 5 more, 5 more, 5 more, 5 more every time.

As the students think back about the different change situations they have encountered, they are identifying some general characteristics of these situations by visualizing their graphs. Through her questions, the teacher helps students focus on why the points on some of the graphs fall in straight lines, while others do not. The students describe how points in a straight line represent a constant rate of change of one variable with respect to the other ("you might get 2 each day, but it doesn't change; you don't start getting 4 a day"). They distinguish between these situations that involve a constant rate of change (linear functions) and situations with varying rates of change, like the growth of plants or the wheelchair race.

Student Math Handbook

The *Student Math Handbook* pages related to this unit are pictured on the following pages. This book is designed to be used flexibly: as a resource for students doing classwork, as a book students can take home for reference while doing homework and playing math games with their families, and as a reference for families to better understand the work their children are doing in class.

When students take the *Student Math Handbook* home, they and their families can discuss these pages together to reinforce or enhance students' understanding of the mathematical concepts and games in this unit.

Graphs

This line graph shows how the temperature changed in Norfolk over time from December 8 to December 14.

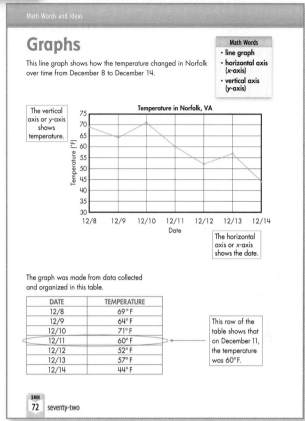

The vertical axis or *y*-axis shows temperature.

The horizontal axis or *x*-axis shows the date.

Math Words
- line graph
- horizontal axis (*x*-axis)
- vertical axis (*y*-axis)

The graph was made from data collected and organized in this table.

DATE	TEMPERATURE
12/8	69° F
12/9	64° F
12/10	71° F
12/11	60° F
12/12	52° F
12/13	57° F
12/14	44° F

This row of the table shows that on December 11, the temperature was 60° F.

SMH 72 seventy-two

Reading Points on a Graph
(page 1 of 2)

Each point on this graph tells us two connected pieces of information, the date and the temperature.

For example, look at the point marked with a star ★ on the graph.

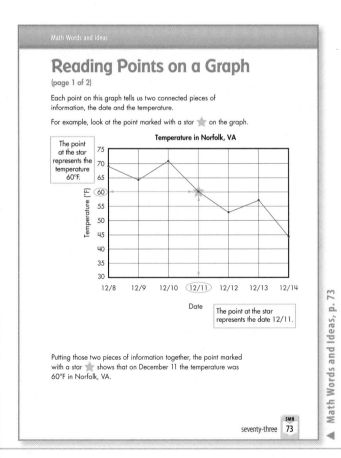

The point at the star represents the temperature 60°F.

The point at the star represents the date 12/11.

Putting those two pieces of information together, the point marked with a star ★ shows that on December 11 the temperature was 60°F in Norfolk, VA.

seventy-three **SMH 73**

Reading Points on a Graph
(page 2 of 2)

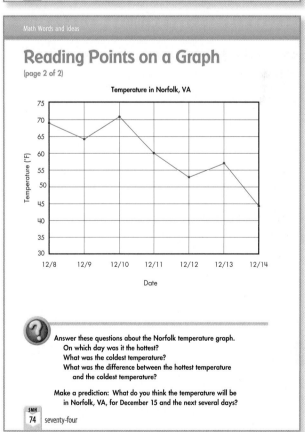

? Answer these questions about the Norfolk temperature graph.
On which day was it the hottest?
What was the coldest temperature?
What was the difference between the hottest temperature and the coldest temperature?

Make a prediction: What do you think the temperature will be in Norfolk, VA, for December 15 and the next several days?

SMH 74 seventy-four

Math Words and Ideas

Telling Stories from Line Graphs (page 1 of 2)

Each of these line graphs represents part of a bicycle race.
The graphs show the speed of the cyclist.

The speed is steady.   *The cyclist rode at a constant speed.*

The speed is increasing.   *The cyclist sped up to pass another rider.*

The speed is decreasing.   *The cyclist slowed down after she crossed the finish line.*

The speed is zero.   *The cyclist stopped to receive her medal.*

◀ Math Words and Ideas, p. 75

seventy-five   **SMH 75**

Math Words and Ideas

Telling Stories from Line Graphs (page 2 of 2)

Here is a graph that represents a complete bicycle race.

Bicycle Race

speeding up A — pedaling steadily B — slowing down C — pedaling steadily D — slowing down to a stop E

Time

Jake wrote this story about the bicycle race.

At the start of the race, the cyclist sped up to her fastest speed. She pedaled steadily at that speed for a while, and then she slowed down. She pedaled steadily at the slower speed for a while. Then she slowed down and stopped at the end of the race.

? Where on the graph is the cyclist's fastest speed?
Look at part B and part D on this graph. What is similar about these parts of the race? What is different?
How many times did the cyclist stop during the bicycle race? How do you know?

SMH 76   seventy-six

◀ Math Words and Ideas, p. 76

Math Words and Ideas

Fast and Slow Growth

These line graphs show how the heights of two different vegetable plants changed over one week.

The heights of both plants increased over the week, but the plants grew at different rates.

Tomato Plant

Su M Tu W Th F Sa
Day of the Week

The tomato plant grew more slowly than the cucumber plant.

Cucumber Plant

Su M Tu W Th F Sa
Day of the Week

The cucumber plant grew more quickly than the tomato plant.

? This graph shows the height of a green bean plant as it grew. Describe the rate of growth of the bean plant over the week.

Green Bean Plant

Su M Tu W Th F Sa
Day of the Week

seventy-seven   **SMH 77**

◀ Math Words and Ideas, p. 77

Math Words and Ideas

The Penny Jar and a Constant Rate of Change

Math Words
- constant rate

In some situations, change happens at a constant rate.

The Penny Jar problems in this unit are situations with a constant rate of change.

The rule for the Penny Jar shown below is:

Start with 3 pennies and add 5 pennies each round.

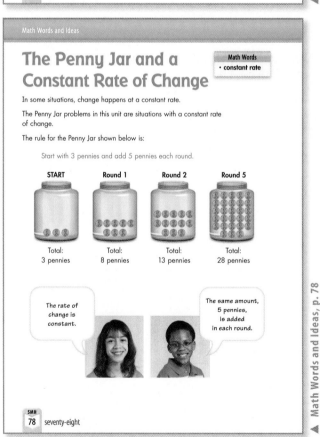

START	Round 1	Round 2	Round 5
Total: 3 pennies	Total: 8 pennies	Total: 13 pennies	Total: 28 pennies

The rate of change is constant.

The same amount, 5 pennies, is added in each round.

SMH 78   seventy-eight

◀ Math Words and Ideas, p. 78

How Many Pennies in the Penny Jar?

For the Penny Jar on page 78, how many pennies will be in the jar after the 4th round?

Jill's solution

Jill drew a picture to find out.

Start with 3 pennies and add 5 pennies each round.

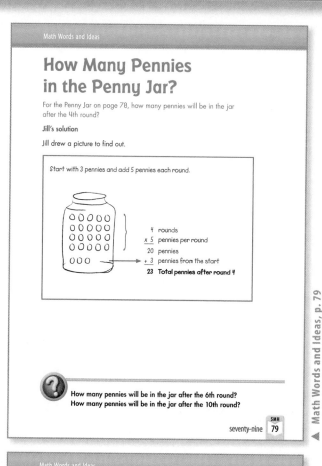

```
 4   rounds
x 5   pennies per round
20   pennies
+ 3   pennies from the start
23   Total pennies after round 4
```

How many pennies will be in the jar after the 6th round?
How many pennies will be in the jar after the 10th round?

seventy-nine **79**

A Table for a Penny Jar Problem

Anna made a table for this Penny Jar problem.

Start with 3 pennies and add 5 pennies each round.

Number of Rounds	Total Number of Pennies
Start	3
1	8
2	13
3	18
4	23
5	28
6	33
7	38
10	53
15	78
20	?

+5 each round

This row shows that after the 4th round there is a total of 23 pennies in the jar.

Beginning here the table skips some rows.

What is the total number of pennies for round 20?
How did you figure that out?

80 eighty

A Graph for a Penny Jar Problem

Marisol made a graph for this Penny Jar problem.

Start with 3 pennies and add 5 pennies each round.

This point represents the 4th round with a total of 23 pennies.

(graph: Number of Pennies vs. Round)

Marisol wondered, "Why are the points in a straight line?"
Why do you think the points on the graph are in a straight line?

eighty-one **81**

Penny Jar Comparisons

(page 1 of 4)

Here are two Penny Jar problems.

Penny Jar A
Start with 6 and add 4 each round.

Penny Jar B
Start with 0 and add 4 each round.

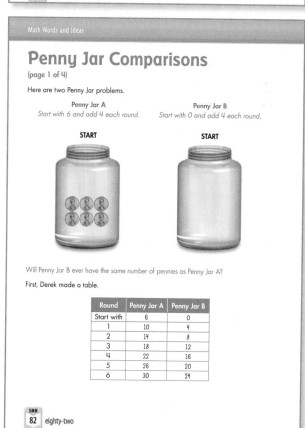

Will Penny Jar B ever have the same number of pennies as Penny Jar A?

First, Derek made a table.

Round	Penny Jar A	Penny Jar B
Start with	6	0
1	10	4
2	14	8
3	18	12
4	22	16
5	26	20
6	30	24

82 eighty-two

Penny Jar Comparisons

(page 2 of 4)

Next, Derek represented the table as a graph.

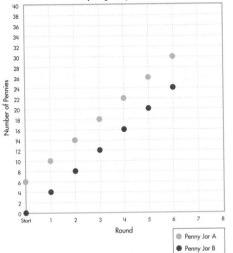

Comparing Penny Jars A and B

(graph: y-axis Number of Pennies 0–40, x-axis Round Start–8)

Legend:
● Penny Jar A
● Penny Jar B

 Will Penny Jar B ever have the same number of pennies as Penny Jar A? How does the table show that? How does the graph show that?

eighty-three **83**

◄ Math Words and Ideas, p. 83

Penny Jar Comparisons

(page 3 of 4)

Here are two Penny Jar problems.

Penny Jar A
Start with 6 and add 4 each round.

Penny Jar C
Start with 4 and add 2 each round.

Will Penny Jar C ever have the same number of pennies as Penny Jar A?

Neomi used a table and a graph to find out.

Round	Penny Jar A	Penny Jar C
Start with	6	4
1	10	6
2	14	8
3	18	10
4	22	12
5	26	14
6	30	16

Comparing Penny Jars A and C

(graph: y-axis Number of Pennies 0–40, x-axis Round 0–8)

Legend:
♦ Penny Jar A
■ Penny Jar C

 Will Penny Jar C ever have the same number of pennies as Penny Jar A? How does the table show that? How does the graph show that?

84 eighty-four

◄ Math Words and Ideas, p. 84

Penny Jar Comparisons

(page 4 of 4)

Here are two Penny Jar problems.

Penny Jar A
Start with 6 and add 4 each round.

Penny Jar D
Start with 0 and add 6 each round.

Will Penny Jar D ever have the same number of pennies as Penny Jar A?

Steve used a table and a graph to find out.

Round	Penny Jar A	Penny Jar D
Start with	6	0
1	10	6
2	14	12
3	18	18
4	22	24
5	26	30
6	30	36

Comparing Penny Jars A and D

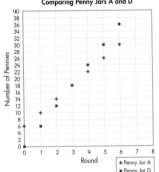

(graph: y-axis Number of Pennies 0–40, x-axis Round 0–8)

Legend:
♦ Penny Jar A
■ Penny Jar D

 Will Penny Jar D ever have the same number of pennies as Penny Jar A? How does the table show that? How does the graph show that?

eighty-five **85**

◄ Math Words and Ideas, p. 85

Writing Rules
to Describe Change

Start with 8 pennies and add 5 pennies each round.

How many pennies will there be in the jar after 10 rounds?

```
    10   rounds
  × 5   pennies per round
   50   pennies


  + 8   pennies from the start
   58   Total pennies after round 10
```

A teacher asked her students to write a rule for the number of pennies for any round, using words or an arithmetic expression.

Luke's rule: You multiply the round number by 5, and then you add 8 because that is the number of pennies in the jar at the beginning.

Steve's rule: Round number x 5 + 8

Sabrina's rule: 8 + (5 x n)

 Can you use one of these rules or your own rule to find out how many pennies will be in the jar after round 30?

Is there ever a round when you will have exactly 200 pennies in this jar? (If so, what round will that be?) How do you know?

86 eighty-six

◄ Math Words and Ideas, p. 86

Index